CONTENTS

Dedicated to our wonderful colleagues at Impact factory who have helped build our magnificent body of personal development work

THE
nice
FACTOR

the art of saying NO

Jo Ellen Grzyb and Robin Chandler

Published in 2008 by Fusion Press,
a division of Satin Publications Ltd
101 Southwark Street
London SE1 0JF
UK

info@visionpaperbacks.co.uk
www.visionpaperbacks.co.uk
Publisher: Sheena Dewan

First published in Great Britain by Simon and Schuster Ltd, 1997

A catalogue record for this book is available from the British Library.

ISBN: 978-1-9054745-36-4

2 4 6 8 10 9 7 5 3

Cover and text design by ok?design

Printed and bound in the UK by
J H Haynes & Co Ltd, Sparkford

Acknowledgements

We give our thanks and acknowledgement to our agent, Leslie Gardner of Artellus Ltd, who is simply brilliant, for her support and superlative guidance. Great thanks go to Sheena Dewan and Louise Coe of Fusion Press for their vision and enthusiasm for our book.

Introduction

In a world where aggression is a common form of communication and violence appears to be on the increase, isn't it a good thing that there are nice people? Don't we need politeness and pleasantness around us more and more? Why would anybody write a book about becoming less nice?

One of the very reasons aggression is on the increase is because, as a culture, we are **too** nice. Every time we swallow a hurt, let someone get away with bad behaviour, give someone the benefit of the doubt or let someone off the hook, we are being too nice. Every time we make excuses for someone, smooth things over, do anything to keep the peace, avoid conflict, then we create a storehouse of anger and resentment that will eventually burst open.

If we are incapable of communicating our thoughts and feelings effectively, then there will inevitably be a backlash of some kind. This inability to articulate the inner world so that it is understood by others in the outer world is why niceness is a crippling liability.

As directors of Impact Factory, a personal development and training company, we have been working for years with all kinds of people in many different stages of their lives on issues to do with communication, personal effectiveness, work and career difficulties and emotional hang-ups, many of which have highlighted the issue of niceness.

We believe that being too nice is a serious problem. When we created our workshops designed to deal with being too nice back in 1993, we touched a nerve that resonated with people in ways we didn't expect. What we found is that we articulated for people a whole range of their behaviour that they had heretofore resignedly accepted, believing there was nothing they could do about it.

We know that there is a cultural context which rewards people for accommodating behaviour. It makes life easier, so we are told, if we turn the other cheek, do unto others as we would have others do unto us and play fair. All quite noble thoughts. However, it's quite unfair in practice if you are unable to choose not to be nice.

Do any of the following scenarios sound familiar?

> Gillian has just settled down for a quiet cup of tea when the phone rings.
>
> 'Hello, Gill, it's me, Angela. I know you're not really busy right now, with the children away at school and your daily there, so I thought it would be a good idea if you picked me up and we went to that new garden centre that's just opened up. I'd take my car but yours is so much bigger we'll get more stuff in it. I'll expect you in a half-hour, OK?'
>
> 'Er. well, I'm not actually doing anything, but I did have some reading I wanted to catch up on and I...'
>
> 'Oh don't be silly. The fresh air will do you good – you don't want to sit alone all day do you? And besides you can read anytime. Bye, see you soon.'

And Gillian gets roped into another outing she doesn't want to go on.

Why not just say no? It's not a difficult word: en oh. But for Gillian, saying no would be like swimming the English Channel before she graduates from the kiddie pool.

What about this?

> 'Hey, Charlie! Glad I caught you before you left the office. Someone has to stay late tonight to wait for a fax that's coming from Los Angeles and it'll need an answer right away. You're always so good at turning around these requests, I really need you to stay.'
>
> 'Well, I can't tonight. My wife's going to her keep-fit class and it's my turn to baby-sit.'

'Whoa! You're not turning into one of those hen-pecked husbands are you? What's more important, the client in LA or your wife's keep-fit class?'

'Um, well, she'll be very upset. I don't want to disappoint her.'

'I'm not really hearing this, am I? You're not the man I thought you were, Charles – the ambitious go-getter, who's angling for the Divisional Manager's job.'

'Well, I guess I could give Trish a call and let her know I'll be a little late.'

'Atta boy, Charlie, I knew I could count on you!'

Oops! Charlie's in the doghouse with a very put-out wife.

And another one:

'Louise, hi, it's Nick.'

'Hi, Nick, is everything still on for tonight?'

'You see, that's why I rang. Something's cropped up with my mother and I won't be able to see you tonight. I'm really sorry but you know how it is...'

'Oh, that's OK. I don't really mind.'

'Are you sure?'

'No, really, it's all right. Of course I don't mind.'

'Well, that's all right then, I'll give you a ring some time. Bye.'

And one furious Louise slams the phone down, raging that she's been let down again.

And this?

'This soup's too cold. I think maybe I should get them to reheat it.'

'No, no, don't make a fuss, what will people think!'

'Yes, but it's not hot enough.'

'Give it to me. I'll eat it. You can have mine.'

'I don't want yours. It'll only take a minute. Waiter!'

'Shh. You're embarrassing me.'

'Yes, but...'

'For my sake, please stop acting so silly. You're so selfish. Why don't you think of others for a change.'

'Oh, all right.'

Cold soup and hot anger are consumed at the same time.

One more:

'Mum, we're not going to be able to come to Sunday lunch this week.'

Silence

'Mum?'

'What do you mean you can't come this Sunday? What's wrong? What's happened? You always come to Sunday lunch. What have I done to upset you?'

'Nothing, Mum. Nothing's wrong and you haven't done anything. I just thought I'd like to spend the day alone with the kids and Joyce for a change.'

'What do you mean, alone? Do I bother you when you're here? Do I crowd you? And what about your father? He hasn't been at all well, you know, and he so looks forward to having his grandchildren around him.'

'Oh, all right, we'll be there around two.'

'No, no, don't put yourself out on my account.'

'It's OK, Mother, we'll be there at two.'

'No, no, if you don't want to be with us one day out of the week, I wouldn't want to force you.'

'Mum, we're coming.'

'Well, if it's what you really want to do, we'll be here waiting as always.'

These are the kind of situations that can create a nasty person out of a nice one. All the while people are asked to do something they do not want to do and they do not voice their feelings or say what they want, then they give in to others, swallow disappointments and feel very resentful. When that resentment builds up and spills over, our too nice people suddenly become overwhelmed by emotion and turn nasty.

They explode inappropriately, they lash out, cause scenes and then, after the shock of it all, retreat right back into being as nice as they ever were and things go back to normal.

For us, these people are too nice for their own good. They give in, they have no resistance in the face of what other people want, they can't stand up for themselves or get what they want.

They don't know how to tell other people that they feel put upon or suffocated or that they are angry or hurt. They're afraid of hurting other people's feelings and of missing out on promotion. They're concerned they'll lose friendships and cause family rifts. They fear they will trigger anger in other people and get yelled at and cause a scene they can't handle.

The fear of consequences is what governs these nice people and limits what they are able to do in their lives. For them, being too nice really is a serious liability.

In this book we aren't interested in turning you from a nice person into a nasty one. On occasion you do that yourself and you know it's not very pleasant. We will be using the terms 'not nice' and 'not nasty' to describe what we see as the middle ground of behaviour, where you have a choice in how you are going to behave.

It is why we have subtitled this book 'The Art of Saying No'. People who are too nice for their own good are too often afraid to, or completely incapable of, saying no. There's often a fear it will sound harsh, dismissive, rude or brusque, so they don't say anything at all. Here we will look at how to turn niceness into an art, helping you to say no, perhaps without ever using the word.

We will look at all aspects of niceness and nastiness and explore ways in which you can change your behaviour so that you are more in charge of what happens rather than being in the grip of emotions that take over and render you helpless and impotent. You do not have to change your whole self. By understanding the choices available to you and making some new choices, you can make a significant difference in your life.

The world needs nice people. It needs the qualities that nice people have: consideration, thoughtfulness, caring, sensitivity. Nice people are often more attuned. They facilitate difficult situations and deal with difficult people that the rest of the world avoids. They tend to see the best in people and are often genuinely interested in making things easier for others.

Nice people are usually very polite, understanding, empathetic and compassionate. They know what it's like to be the underdog and are genuinely sympathetic. They are usually very welcoming and generous.

Becoming less nice does not mean having to give up all those wonderful qualities that contribute to the world's well-being. Becoming less nice contributes to your well-being.

Jo Ellen and Robin: A Personal Context

The interesting point for us is that we didn't sit around looking for a new subject for a workshop. We created workshops dealing with 'niceness' only after we identified niceness as a difficulty that both of us had and that we wanted to do something about. It was in looking at our own niceness that we realised how rich the subject was.

If you met either of us in person, nice is not the first word that would spring to mind in describing us. We are warm and pleasant people, yes, but seemingly very direct and forthright. Indeed, we would not have considered ourselves lacking in confidence in the least until we began to look at this subject in earnest.

It was only when we began observing the contrast between how we saw ourselves (clear, straightforward, courageous even) and what our behaviour often actually said (adaptive, caretaking, accommodating) that we realised there was a gap that occurred when we felt obliged to be 'nice' about something when we didn't want to be. We seemed unable to close the gap.

There were times when we were unable to speak our minds, when we adapted our behaviour to suit others, when we made someone else's unacceptable behaviour all right for fear of offending.

And it was then that we realised that if we, who hadn't even been aware of the extent of our own difficulties, were, on occasion, too nice for our own good, then there must be thousands of other people who had similar, if not even greater, problems with this issue than we did.

The Nice Factor workshop didn't grow out of our understanding of the problem: it sprang! We created the workshop in an afternoon because the solutions were so straightforward and because we knew that there was nothing particularly deep or psychological about excessive niceness. There was nothing hidden or buried that had to take years of uncovering and probing.

You know when you're being too nice. You may know at the time or later in the day or in three weeks. But however long it takes you to realise you've done something you wish you hadn't, agreed to something you disagreed with, backed down from an argument because you thought you were losing – you know it!

You have long discussions in your head about what you could have done or should have said. You imagine what you might do the next time you're in a similar situation, even though you end up not doing it.

For us, knowing and understanding the issue didn't make dealing with it that much easier. We had to look at far more than 'how to' in order to deal effectively with the problem. Not everyone is too nice in the same way, and the best place for us to start was with our own particular brand of niceness and to then see how we could relate that to a broader picture.

Here, then, are our own stories:

Jo Ellen: I have always thought of myself as thoughtful and sensitive, but I would never have considered that there were parts of my behaviour that were a serious liability. All my life I have been able to stand my ground in the face of authority. I do not intimidate easily: when I'd encountered bullying at work, it took a while but I figured out what to do to combat it and did that by myself.

Therefore, it genuinely shocked me when I realised that there was a whole area of my life that was a complete blind spot which I had ignored: when I entered a personal relationship the strong, confident, direct woman disappeared and this accommodating, adaptive, meek and powerless person emerged.

I had married relatively young (19) to a lovely man who was even nicer than I was, so I never encountered that particular problem during my marriage and therefore didn't have any idea of what was to come after my divorce.

A number of years went by before I had another relationship through most of which I was unhappy and only vaguely understood why. I broke it off after eight months with a feeling of relief. And then another few years went by. By this time I thought I needed to try tackling relationships again. What a disaster! I met plenty of men, and had a couple of flings and found myself disturbed and unhappy most of the time. Having considered myself a relatively happy person, I couldn't quite understand why every time I started to see someone regularly I became just the opposite and I found myself overwhelmed by feelings of helplessness. It didn't make sense.

I'd meet a man and he'd call the shots. Every time I started a relationship, the man decided when we'd see each other, what the parameters of the relationship were and I went along with it. It was such automatic behaviour that I didn't know I was doing it. Except in my head I'd be muttering: 'Why is he deciding when we see each other? I hate sitting by the phone waiting for it to ring; why can't we both phone each other?'

And yet, there I was at 44 years old, sitting by the phone and feeling enraged and powerless to do anything to change my situation. Not only that, I would concoct elaborate fantasies of myself becoming this incredibly cool, sophisticated woman who could toss off phrases like: 'You'll ring me? Oh, I wouldn't bother. Men who say that are usually spineless creeps, so I'm not really interested in someone like you.' Thus killing two birds with one stone: discharging my anger and feeling in control of the situation.

Did I ever do that? What do you think?

It came to a head one particular Christmas. I had been seeing a lot of one man but something crucial was missing which I couldn't put my finger on right away. I liked him and yet again I found myself unhappy most of the time: I couldn't figure it out. And again, with a sense of relief, I decided to break the relationship off. When I returned to work the following week, having thought it all through, I said to Robin, 'That's it! I've had enough! I'm sick and tired of getting myself into this situation time and time again. I'm too nice!'

And the light bulb went on.

Indeed, it was only months after creating The Nice Factor workshop that it occurred to me that one of the reasons I stayed out of relationships at all was so that I wouldn't have to suffer these feelings of helplessness and anxiety. I had created a huge blind spot in my life that I didn't have to face by simply avoiding the cause instead of confronting it. If I'm not in a relationship, then I'm in control; if I'm in a relationship, someone else is in control. Again, it was impossible for me to see any middle ground: all that was visible to me were the extremes.

As well, I was quite quick to say over and over again: 'What's wrong with me?' I believed that only arrogant, unkind men were attracted to me and took it completely to heart when one of my sisters said to me, 'Face it, Jo Ellen, you're a loser magnet.' I didn't know how very true that was: the nicer my behaviour, the stronger the pull to attract men I felt unable to be myself with and say what I felt.

Robin: My awareness coincided with Jo Ellen's but came from a different angle. It was Christmas. Now, I'm not a great fan of Christmas as it is often experienced: a time when families who don't particularly like each other get together for two or more days and are deliberately nice to each other. It seemed ludicrous to me that people came together pretending to enjoy themselves when they'd rather be doing something else. The notion that because it's Christmas, we are supposed to like people we don't really like seemed a big waste of time.

Besides that, whatever false feelings are holding the event together in the first place usually begin to fall apart by Boxing Day when someone gets drunk and makes a scene or when one of the children breaks someone else's favourite toy – then the whole charade falls apart. Christmas is that time of year when many people pretend to have feelings they don't have and eventually the cracks show.

Now this particular Christmas was also a time when a friend (who admittedly can be can be direct and upfront in a way that can make people uncomfortable) had been told by her therapist that she'd get on better in life if she was just a little nicer. That really rubbed me up the wrong way. Why should she be just a little nicer? What she was being told was to change her behaviour to make other people comfortable, and her life would be easier.

But what I also realised was that it was easier for me to get upset on my friend's behalf than it was to get upset on my own. I didn't get nearly as angry when someone tried to get me to change my behaviour and do something I didn't want to do. I realised that I was a lot nicer than I had originally thought!

And on top of that, I also realised that I had the knack of anticipating what other people wanted before they even knew it themselves. I was on 'red alert' to figure out what was needed long before there was any need to do so.

For us it seemed fated that we would create a new workshop designed to deal with these difficulties, having both come to our own separate awareness at the same time: it was a coincidence too good to let pass.

The workshop and the book

Just a bit of a note about our workshops: at the time we created The Nice Factor workshops, we resisted calling them 'assertiveness' workshops because we felt that assertiveness had a bit of a bad name and seemed mostly geared for women. Since 1993 we have evolved, and we now do call our once Nice Factor workshops, Assertiveness. They are for men and women and continue to be one of the most popular programmes we do.

This book brings together the wealth of information, problems, solutions, techniques and tools we have learned over the years so that we might share them. This book is not just for the people who have come along to participate in our workshops, but for anyone who recognises that they, too, have had enough and are ready to change their behaviour to become less nice.

This book is for all types of nice people: from those who simply need a little fine-tuning, to people who feel that they have no control whatsoever when it comes to being taken advantage of.

It is also for other professionals: therapists and counsellors, human resources personnel, management trainers and others who encounter people with these difficulties on a day-to-day basis.

We have been asked on a number of occasions, 'Isn't this really a women's issue?' Emphatically, our answer is NO. Our experience is that this is a problem that exists across the board. Men and women may manifest their niceness differently (although not always) but it is not a problem that's exclusive to one gender. Nor is it exclusive to the British, to specific classes or educational backgrounds.

There is no specific profile we could draw from our years of working with nice people. We work with businessmen and women who have come to a dead end in their professions because they are perceived as not being tough enough to handle the next stage; who hide in their offices rather than confront problems they don't feel they can handle; who always end up taking on extra work because they want to be seen as a good team member.

We work with housewives and mothers who spend all their time doing the school-run for everyone in the neighbourhood, baking for the local fêtes, having Aunt Helen stay for a week when they thought she was coming for a day. These are women other people get impatient with when they dither and can't make up their minds right away; who are perpetually tired because there's never enough time to do everything they think they are supposed to do.

We work with men and women who feel impotent and useless much of the time as they give in yet again to what other people want and live with a low-grade level of depression.

We work with students, retirees, people who run their own businesses, secretaries, lawyers, married couples, accountants, therapists, actors, architects, computer programmers, government workers, NHS personnel – the list goes on and on.

Our clientele is British, Irish, American, Asian, Australian, New Zealand, South African, German, French, Italian, Spanish, Swedish, Canadian, Arab, Cuban, Ghanaian, with an age range from 20 to 60 plus.

If niceness on any level gets in your way, this book will help you.

Briefly, we have divided *The Nice Factor* into two parts:

Part 1: Setting the scene

A chance for you to assess just how nice you are: identifying how you got this way in the first place and putting it in context for the whole of your life; how unspoken rules and behavioural expectations influenced your future behaviour and feelings. This is a chance for you to trace your own specific route to niceness. We look at your behaviour and feelings when you find yourself doing something you don't want to do and how these feelings prevent you from changing the outcome of difficult situations.

We examine the two extremes of behaviour which we call nice and nasty and then describe the alternatives that are available including being 'not nice' and 'not nasty'.

Part 2: Getting your choice back

This is about practising change.

We start with a look at the language of niceness and how language shapes our lives and continues to keep us in our place. We then look at how you can begin to put small 'wins' into effect right away.

The rest of the book includes useful methods, ideas and techniques that you can practise with. We explore status as a way to change your behaviour at will, while keeping some of those difficult feelings at bay; effective boundary setting and conflict resolution.

By having a range of possible options, you can choose the most appropriate methods for you.

This is not a rule book but a chance to look at everything that's available for you to choose from.

Our intention is to take you through a process of recognition and acknowledgement; understanding and action. Recognition and acknowledgement of your specific problem of being too nice and in which areas of your life it is a liability. Understanding how you came to be this way and to see that there is a choice in the way you behave.

And finally, action in seeing what can be done about it, and how to practise the art of saying no.

We provide a process for you to gain insight into the kind of changes that would make your life work better. We have a saying at Impact Factory: 'Let's find the least amount of change for the greatest amount of impact.' We hope that you will use this book to identify manageable ways to make changes in your life that you know are possible – rather than giving yourself a hard time because you can't become assured and strong, the way you are 'supposed' to be, overnight.

Finally, and for us, most importantly, we would like this process of change to be fun – not necessarily side-splitting fun, but an opportunity for bringing some gentle humour into the proceedings. When you are caught on the downside of being too nice, it can feel deadly serious and quite hopeless. The ability to see the humour in situations, to see the ridiculous in other people's behaviour and to be able to laugh at one's self are all ways to take the sting out of doing things differently.

Note: Although we will be dealing with this in greater detail later, it is important to note that this book could just as easily be subtitled *The Nasty Factor*. The source of nice behaviour is a deep-seated belief that you aren't going to get what you want unless you alter yourself (and of course, most of the time that doesn't work). Well, with nasty people, the same is true: they, too, don't think they're going to get what they want and so they will bully and demand and give people a hard time to ensure that they do.

The source is the same; the way it is manifested is different.

PART 1

SETTING THE SCENE

INTRODUCTION

'Setting the scene' is a chance for you to gain some insight and awareness into how being too nice affects you personally. You may find that
the difficulties of this problem are so overwhelming that it is hard to see
how to unravel all the strands that entangle you. On the other hand,
niceness may not be such a big problem for you but it may create
enough small difficulties that cannot be ignored.

Although for some of you it may feel a very complex problem, it isn't
deeply complicated. There are aspects of your behaviour which don't
work well for you, and you know this.

We hope that this book offers an accessible perspective on this issue,
presenting you with an opportunity to identify:

- the ways in which you manifest niceness
- the primary sources of your adaptive behaviour
- the feelings that keep you limited and stuck

We look at the entire range of behaviour available to you which you
may be aware of on one level but feel incapable of accessing.

We encourage you to do as many of the exercises as you can and if
possible to keep a journal of some nature to record some of the feelings,
thoughts and ideas that are stimulated by the exercises and questions
asked in the next four chapters.

Our aim throughout the entire book, but especially in Part 1, is to
stimulate your thinking so that you can gain a greater perspective on
and insight into the whole issue of being too nice for your own good.

Since a great deal of your limiting behaviour was learned, it can be 'unlearned'. We hope that through the material we present here you will be able to clarify some of your thinking and feeling and develop your niceness from being a liability to becoming an asset.

1

ARE YOU TOO NICE FOR YOUR OWN GOOD?

You have been given a ticket for a sold-out concert of your favourite group, but it's on the same night as your mother's birthday dinner.
Do you:

a. Go to your mother's dinner, not mention the concert, and possibly feel resentful?
b. Lie and tell her you have to work late on an emergency, there was nothing you could do about it and you're really, really sorry?
c. Tell her straight out that you have a dilemma and you've decided to go to the concert and you'll celebrate her birthday the next evening?

Your best friend asks you to take care of his dog while he's away for a week because you work freelance and will be home all day. You don't exactly dislike his dog but it's not that well house-trained outside its own home and you hate cleaning up after it.
Do you:

a. Say it's no bother at all, take the dog and put newspapers all over your carpeting?
b. Say you'd love to but you're having workmen in the whole week and everything's going to be disrupted so it's not possible to have it?
c. Tell him the truth about your difficulty with the dog's untrained habits and say you don't want to do it?

You're lying in bed with your new partner, kissing and cuddling prior to making love. You know exactly what you'd like him to do to really turn you on.

Do you:

a. Lie there and hope he'll figure it out?
b. Do it to him first in the hope he'll get the idea and do it back?
c. Tell him what turns you on and how much you'd like him to do it?

You are a computer whizz. At the office you once went out of your way to help someone with some personal work on your computer because she doesn't use one for her job. Now she keeps coming back pleading with you to help her out which means accommodating her personal needs in your work-time or may even mean staying late.

Do you:

a. Smile a lot, say it's OK, you don't mind at all helping her out and stay a couple of hours late to finish her work for her?
b. Tell her the computer's crashed and there's now a backlog of work and you can't fit her work in?
c. Tell her you were happy to have done one favour for her, but that any more would be out of the question?

Our first reaction to the above dilemmas is to assume that there is a right way to handle them. If you know you're too nice for your own good, you'll probably recognise the first and second solutions as the kind you've taken time and time again. And you may imagine that if only you were strong and assertive then the correct way to behave would be by choosing solution c every time. WRONG.

With behaviour there is no right or wrong way to be. There is no formula or set of rules that you can rely on at all times and for all situations. It is hard not to wish for something solid to hang onto which tells you that you are going in the right direction.

The challenge of this book is to help you identify the behavioural changes that you can cope with. As an adaptive person you will probably have exceptionally high expectations of how you are supposed to conduct your life. You may be extremely self-critical and when you are unable to change the way you communicate and behave with other people, you feel a failure.

We do not want to encourage the kind of thinking that contributes to more failure: eg the right way to behave is to always be direct; the wrong way to behave is to always be meek and mild.

This book is not going to provide you with the **right** way, but rather with **another** way; with quite a few other ways, in fact. The choice will always rest with you as to which way is right for which situation.

We use the term 'nice' because it so accurately describes the kind of behaviour that causes people to feel cut off from their true selves and their true inclinations and impulses. But 'nice' behaviour is not necessarily wrong. Later in the book we will be exploring how to use your 'nice' behaviour to your own best advantage.

Nice: a weak modifier

The primary dictionary definition of 'nice' is hard to please, precise, careful, minutely accurate, having high standards. However, in current cultural terms, 'nice' is used to mean pleasant, agreeable and considerate.

For the purposes of this book, and the definition which has underscored The Nice Factor workshop, we see it as rather a bland and dull word which implies lack of substance and forcefulness. The spellcheck on our computer chides us for its overuse, calling it a weak modifier. People often use the word when they can't think of anything else to say: 'Oh, that's a nice dress you're wearing.' 'What a nice person he is.' 'You did a nice job on the ABC project.'

For us, 'nice' is the end of the spectrum of possible behaviour where people are ineffective, invisible, adaptive and powerless. We do not think being nice is wrong. It can be a lovely way to behave: it can mean being sensitive, thoughtful, caring, understanding and attentive to the needs of others. There are times when it is very important to be accommodating, pleasant and agreeable.

However, this becomes a problem when you are too attentive, too thoughtful, too agreeable, too understanding. It becomes a problem when you don't feel you have a choice in how you behave and are therefore nice when you would rather act differently. Then it usually means impotence, unspoken frustration, low-level depression and a real sense of something being not quite right.

If it is appropriate to be polite, pleasing and accommodating then 'nice' behaviour is fine. In the face of being bullied, ridiculed, insulted or simply misunderstood it is appropriate to be direct and forceful. However, if fear of not being liked or of offending or of triggering someone's anger stops you from acting in your own best interests, then 'nice' behaviour is most certainly a liability.

People who are too nice really do believe that they have no choice in the matter. They think, 'Well, this is just the way I am and there's nothing I can do about it.' They get trampled upon because they no longer have access (or believe that they have no access) to alternative forms of behaviour which could stop this happening.

We all of us do things at times that we'd rather not. That's part of being a social animal. We live in a variety of communities: the communities of family, home, work, neighbourhood, town, country, etc. And of course there will be occasions when we put aside our wants and needs to contribute to the larger community.

That could mean agreeing to stay late at work one evening in order to get a mailing completed, even though you'd rather be out with your friends at your local. It could mean attending the Christmas fête and buying more jars of jam than you could possibly need in order to feel part of your local church or village, even though you hate social gatherings of any kind.

You might forfeit a round of golf to go shopping with your wife for bedroom curtains; you might skip the yoga class to visit Aunt Rose and her aged, smelly dog; you might grit your teeth and get dressed up to go to a gala sponsored by your husband's company when you'd rather be watching *EastEnders*, you might listen to a good friend wailing about her latest relationship debacle just when you were about to sit down to dinner; you might 'volunteer' for a Boy Scout event because your son really wants you there, when you'd rather have a peaceful Saturday at home.

None of these is really a great hardship and although you might feel put out because you'd rather be doing something else or don't want to be bothered, they are minor sacrifices for the greater good of your job, your marriage, your family relations, your friendships. They are irritations that are well balanced by the goodwill they create in others and the sense of having made a deposit in the bank of good deeds which supports our self-esteem.

However, when these kind of 'sacrifices' are the norm instead of the exception to how you run your life, then the balance is out of kilter: the withdrawals far outweigh the deposits. Soon the bank of goodwill is completely used up and is beginning to be filled with resentment and disappointment, which causes an erosion of self-esteem.

In addition, if you are too nice, and we mean really too nice, people don't like you anyway. You frustrate them: they want to shake you because of your indecisiveness, your feeble rejoinders, your weak opinions. When you say 'Whatever you want is OK with me' or 'I don't mind' some people will metaphorically throw up their hands in disgust because they can't stand the passivity.

Just how nice are you?

It is important for you to define where you find your behaviour beneficial and where you find it a liability. See where you fit into the wide spectrum of our definition of nice behaviour. Study the following list of some of the things that adaptive people do. It will help you identify for yourself the areas where you find it difficult to be anything but accommodating and the areas where you feel you are in balance and have a say in the outcome of the transaction.

This is a chance for you to self-assess the degree to which you modify your natural inclinations and to identify some of the feelings you get when you do modify your behaviour when you don't want to.

We can't stress forcefully enough that none of the behaviours listed below are right or wrong. Only if you recognise it as a liability, is it one. For instance, avoiding conflict at any cost might be perfectly all right for some people and never cause them any problems at all. While for others, avoiding conflict means they never get to disagree, never manage to stand up for themselves, never have the experience of achieving a successful conclusion to a confrontation – and then they end up feeling bad.

We are often too quick to judge our actions: this is good or that is bad. If you personally identify something as a problem then it is a problem for you. It may not be a problem for someone else. Therefore, to declare that all overly nice behaviour is wrong would be a mistake on our part.

This book is for you to determine where you have difficulties and what you can do to alleviate them. It is not to make a whole new set of rules about the correct way to run your lives!

Here are our self-assessment questions. Next to each question mark: 1 for Never, 2 for Occasionally, 3 for Often, and 4 for Always.

Do you:

- Apologise even when you haven't done anything wrong?
- Ask for permission when it's unnecessary – for instance: 'Is it OK if I make a cup of tea?'
- Avoid conflict at any cost?
- Assume everything is your fault every time something goes wrong?
- Worry about what other people think, even if you don't even know them?
- Lie to get out of doing something you don't want to do and then hide, afraid of being caught out in the lie?
- Want to be liked by everyone, even though you don't like everyone?
- Find it impossible to say 'no'?
- Feel you need to make everything all right for other people?
- Expect people to be as considerate as you are?
- Give in to what other people want?
- Make excuses for someone else's bad or thoughtless behaviour?
- Feel guilty when you ask for something you want?
- Smile when you are giving or receiving bad news?
- Feel responsible for cheering people up when they're unhappy?
- Fear being ridiculed if you speak your mind?
- Imagine you know what other people are thinking?
- Expect others to judge you badly rather than thinking well of you?
- Try to be the peacemaker when other people are arguing?
- Believe people don't want to hear what you have to say?

- Avoid being the centre of attention for fear of being accused of showing off?
- Justify your behaviour if someone questions something you do?
- Swallow hurts without letting others know they've upset you?
- Expect to be told off if you haven't followed what you think are the rules?
- Feel intimidated and wish that you hadn't picked up the phone when one of your parents rings up?
- Make decisions based on what you think other people expect of you?
- Act the clown to lighten difficult situations which you're not sure how to handle?
- Apologise on behalf of people close to you when they've done something you think other people won't like?
- Ask redundant questions such as: 'Can I ask a question?' or 'Would it be all right if...?'
- Feel unable to tell people you are close to how you are feeling?
- Take it personally when someone is making a general criticism?
- Agree to things because they're expected of you?
- Agree to things because you think they're expected of you?
- Rage inside while smiling on the outside when you get angry?
- Feel unable to tell your partner what you want sexually?
- Get angry about little things but don't mention the big issues?
- Hate asking for favours?
- Go on holidays to places you don't want to visit because everyone else wants to go there?
- Lend money and then feel unable to ask for it back?
- Have friends who overstay their welcome?
- Feel that it's not all right to change your mind?
- Receive lots of advice along the lines of 'The best thing for you to do is...'?
- Find it impossible to tell your best friends they've upset you?
- Expect to be told off when someone says 'There's something I have to tell you'?
- Get roped into outings you don't want because you don't have a 'good' excuse handy?
- Feel you have to remember everybody's birthday?

- Feel guilty when you ask for and get something you want?
- Lose your temper unexpectedly over seemingly unimportant things?
- Do the washing-up or cleaning-up after your flatmate/ partner/ children?
- Get stuck with the school-run most mornings?
- Feel anxious if you delay returning something you've borrowed?
- Agree even when you don't?
- Overbook your commitments?
- Take the path of least resistance because it's easier than fighting?
- Feel you're not good enough?
- Get overlooked for promotion?
- Over-apologise when you're late?
- (If you drive) imagine that the driver behind you is critical of your driving?
- Seek confirmation when you make a suggestion – for example: 'Is that all right with you'?
- Say 'You shouldn't have' when people give you gifts?
- Get asked to stay late at work or do work nobody else wants to do?
- Find it impossible to take the initiative at meetings?
- Attract criticism and rarely praise from colleagues and bosses?
- Find yourself saying 'Whatever you want to do is fine with me' when someone asks you what you want to do?
- Find it hard to accept compliments gracefully?
- Get bullied at work?
- Wait to be offered a raise instead of asking for one?
- Undercharge for your services if you're freelance?
- Find it difficult to break routines?
- Feel you have to go to every party you're invited to?
- Eat food you don't like rather than send it back?
- Put up with unwanted noise rather than ask someone to stop using their mobile phone, iPod, etc?
- Replay conversations in your head over and over?
- Replay conversations in your head that you haven't even had yet?
- Feel unable to return an item you've bought because you don't like it, rather than because there is something wrong with it?

- Get stuck with the party bore?
- Feel you're not allowed to have an 'off' day?
- Give your phone number to people you never want to see again?
- Get told that you're too sensitive?
- Hedge your bets by telling other people what's wrong with you before they have a chance to say it to you first?
- Feel guilty because you think you ought to love your parents more?

Evaluating your responses

Manageable

If most of your answers are 1s and 2s (Never or Occasionally), then you probably are a good judge of the appropriate behaviour for a particular situation. You may sometimes do things you'd rather not or mentally kick yourself for altering your behaviour when you wish you hadn't. But in general, your life probably works the way you'd like it to.

You're not afraid of being disliked because you know it's impossible for everyone to like everyone and therefore it is unlikely you feel compelled to alter your behaviour to make others happy. You are well-integrated, which means that your inner and outer worlds match. You don't edit your thoughts and actions to such a degree that you diminish yourself.

This book will be useful for you to help you fine-tune those few uncomfortable areas of your life you'd like to be more in charge of. It will help you sharpen up some dulled responses and allow you to have some fun while doing so.

Borderline

If most of your answers are 2s and 3s (Occasionally and Often) then there are most likely some areas in your life that don't work as well as you'd like and where situations feel as though they are in someone else's control. For you, niceness doesn't rule your life, but it exerts a fairly strong influence and you'd like to be able to readjust aspects of your behaviour that are stopping you feeling comfortable with yourself.

It may seem that life is made up of contradictions: at times you have no problem sticking up for yourself, getting what you want, going against the status quo and feeling comfortable doing so; and then there will be other times when you buckle under, feel too paralysed with indecision to do anything and/or get angry without voicing your feelings.

Since you know there are times when you can affect the outcome of tricky situations in your favour and other times when you seem powerless to change anything, it will be the contradictions which are most puzzling.

This book will help you to resolve those contradictions and to bring more balance into your life. It will help you to become better adjusted and less at the mercy of others. You already have a clear picture of how you'd like your life to be; this book will help you complete the picture.

Problematic

If most of your answers are 3s and 4s (Often and Always), then you already know how serious this is for you.

You know you feel compromised and let down a lot of the time. Your head says 'No' but your mouth says 'Yes'. You're afraid of offending and continually adapt your behaviour to suit what you **think** other people want. You are probably a people-pleaser because you fear that not pleasing could somehow land you in a great deal of trouble. You play the game of life by rules you've made up. Not only that, you really do believe these rules are in other people's control.

You feel uncomfortable a lot of the time: uneasy, unsure, anxious, frustrated and worried. And then you think that you should not be feeling this way; that it's silly or pathetic and that you ought to pull yourself together. Your level of compassion for yourself is often nil and you imagine other people think you're pathetic as well. In truth, it really isn't as bad as you may think it is.

This book will help you feel less bad about your plight. It will show you that you are not alone in feeling overwhelmed by your emotions and unable to affect some of the difficult situations that you desperately want to change. You are not a hopeless case. There are many people who suffer in similar ways. You do not have to be a doormat any longer!

What were your feelings?

Being able to evaluate your behaviour is only step one and is useful only insofar as it helps you identify your problem areas. There is much more to this nice business than your behaviour.

Chapter 3 is devoted entirely to looking at the feelings that occur when you are caught between wanting to do one thing and finding yourself doing another, and we will encourage you to recognise and register the range of emotions you experience as you are reading through the book.

However, for starters, let's look at the feelings you had when you answered the questions. Was there any noticeable pattern of response? Are you at your most adaptive when it comes to family situations or friends or work? Is there one area that stands out as causing you the most difficulty or are there many?

Was there anything that surprised you? Perhaps in some areas you're not as nice as you thought you were and in others you're **much** nicer than you thought. How would you feel if someone else read your list?

What were your feelings as you numbered your responses? Did you feel uncomfortable? Were you embarrassed or ashamed? Relieved that other people might have similar difficulties to yours? Did you giggle? Cringe? Go numb? Find yourself losing concentration?

Did you say, 'I used to do that, but I don't any more' or just the opposite: 'I never did that before, and now I find myself doing it again and again'?

Did you chide yourself and say, 'This is really all nonsense, and all I have to do is be stronger next time' or did you breathe a sigh of relief that help might finally be on the way?

Because being agreeable is so applauded in this culture, many people feel selfish about doing anything other than what they have always done. Selfish is a word quite often used to get people to modify their behaviour. And it works! There is a general feeling that to be selfish is a 'bad' thing and to be selfless is a 'good' thing.

Poor nice people, who never get a real chance to find out what it feels like to be selfish, to put their own needs first for a change.

You're only as big as the box that you're in

Every time you change your behaviour, when you feel you have no choice in the matter, you limit your expressiveness. You can only be spontaneous if you are not constantly on guard and concerned about the effect your actions are having on other people.

Putting limits on yourself is not wrong. If you didn't, what an anarchistic, chaotic society we would live in! Then the term selfish really would mean self-indulgent and self-seeking. The world would be populated by six-foot children with no sense of social responsibility.

However, if the emotions that govern your life are fed by insecurity, shame, humiliation and fear of criticism, then the range of behaviour that is available to you is very narrow. If you are ruled by fear, this will keep you small and will feed your low self-esteem.

Think about it: the last time you wanted to do something outside your normal range of behaviour, what went on in your head? There might have been a running monologue that included such phrases as: 'I couldn't possibly do that!' 'You ought to know better.' 'They won't like it.' 'She'll be really insulted.' 'He'll really be upset.'

With this running commentary you edit down the possibilities and thereby feel hampered about doing any of the things you might really want to do. For example:

- 'If I tell my mother not to phone me every night, she'll be really hurt; and I could never hurt my mother.'
- 'If I tell my girlfriend I like her better with long hair, she'll never speak to me again.'
- 'If I tell my boss I'm struggling with the Henderson report, he'll think I'm useless and never give me anything important to do again.'
- 'If I eat the last cake on the plate, everyone will think I'm over-indulgent and out of control.'
- 'If I tell them I didn't like the film we went to see on Friday, they'll think I have no taste and they won't be friends with me any more.'

In each of these 'If I ...' situations two things are apparent: first, it is the fear of consequences that stops us from acting or speaking spontaneously; second, we tend to think in worst-case scenarios.

We rarely think, 'If I tell my boss I'm having trouble with the Henderson project, he'll probably get someone else in to help.' Or, 'If I tell my boss I'm having trouble with the Henderson report, he'll try to find out where my problem is and find a solution.' We box ourselves in and the box is usually very small. It is filled with rules, shoulds and musts.

Am I the only one?

There are many ways in which nice people manifest their niceness and we won't describe them all. Throughout this book we will be using case histories based on the life stories we have heard: they are our own stories, the lives we've heard about on our workshop and histories from other people we've met over the years and talked to about this issue. Names have been changed to protect the nice.

We are very moved that people have opened their hearts and lives to us and talked so touchingly of their difficulties. We know that it is when we are at our most personal that we can touch others with empathy and compassion. We hope that in using these stories to depict both the problems and the solutions that you will be able to gain some insight into your own personal situations.

Here are a few examples which make clear how very defeating adaptive behaviour can be.

I want to be alone

Most, if not all, people are truly themselves when they are by themselves. They do little to modify their behaviour because there isn't the probability of being seen and of being judged. Thus, they sing uninhibitedly while dusting the furniture, put their feet on the sofa while watching a football match, swear like a trooper when they stub a toe, eat with their fingers and lick their plates, eat straight from the saucepan instead of using dishes, leave dirty clothes lying around and so on.

As soon as one other person comes into the equation, you will naturally change your behaviour. Some of that change is understandable and useful. For instance, in this culture we have determined that it is antisocial to pick your nose in public. A lot of you do it anyway when you're alone. Far fewer of you do it when you are with someone else. That's accepted social behaviour and there is nothing wrong with that kind of modification: it maintains an accepted status quo without really infringing on your true self.

However, if you are someone who modifies your behaviour because of the fear of being judged, ridiculed or shamed, then you are working to a set of your own rules that have not been agreed to by other people (they haven't been consulted).

Here is an example:

Jean is 26. When on her own, Jean is a rather flamboyant, playful person. She likes pulling silly faces in front of the mirror, she dances with reckless abandon to her favourite songs, accompanying them loudly and off-key. She concocts 'I wonder if this will work' type of meals which she often flushes down the loo. She has endless conversations with her cat, Mimi, whom she is certain understands every word and whom she lets sit on the table while she eats. Her comfortable clothes are baggy trousers and Day-Glo sweatshirts. She has her favourite stuffed teddy bear on her bed. She is a passionate supporter of Greenpeace and has a Rainbow Warrior poster on one of her walls.

Jean started to date Ed, a man she met through work, and after a couple of weeks invited him to dinner. She agonised over just the right kind of meal to cook. She dressed demurely in a skirt and blouse, hid her teddy bear and her Greenpeace poster and locked the cat in the bedroom.

When he started talking politics she smiled a lot and agreed with whatever he said. She agreed it was probably a bad idea to keep animals in a flat when they'd be much happier outside. She even said she'd love to go to the opera with him, though she can't stand it. When he commented that he thought she looked good, she said she thought it was important for clothes to reflect the true inner person and she was always more comfortable wearing something feminine.

Inside, part of her couldn't believe what was coming out of her mouth! Was this really her talking? But a much stronger part of her was certain that if she disagreed with him, told him she wouldn't let her cat outside in a hundred years, hated wearing skirts and hated opera even more, then he wouldn't like her.

Without any evidence, Jean had already decided exactly how she was supposed to behave in order to be acceptable to Ed. She had created a whole set of rules about what was acceptable and what wasn't and thus compromised who she really was. She didn't think that who she really was was OK.

Jean's story is one of many where there is a huge discrepancy between the person she is when she is most herself and the person she becomes when she fears she's going to be judged and found wanting.

Dr Jekyll and Mr Hyde: the kicking the cat syndrome

Then there are the people who appear to have split personalities. At work they are one person, at home another. Neither one is the person they want to be, but they seem to have no control over how they behave in either place.

Here's an example:

At home, Tim is a forceful, opinionated middle-aged man. He knows exactly how his favourite football team should be managed; he could sort out the government in an afternoon. He likes nothing more than to commentate angrily at the news as it's being read out. He has strong views about how his two children should be raised and has long, loud arguments with his wife about the proper way to bring up his offspring; and he'll tell the teachers so if given the chance.

He's exhausted when he gets home from work and loses his temper at the slightest provocation, so everyone knows to stay out of his way till he gets back from a visit to the pub. At his local, his mates have fun winding him up because he can be baited so easily. He pretends to take it all good-naturedly but sometimes he wishes he could get into a fight so he could let off some steam.

At work, Tim is transformed. He never opens his mouth. If he's asked to make a presentation he finds ingenious ways to avoid doing so. If he's asked his opinion at meetings he tries to work out all the angles to see what opinion will go down well with his employers. He has more work than he can handle but instead of asking for help or a reassessment of his workload, he stays late most evenings to catch up. This is why he is so tired at the end of the day and has no time for his family.

Tim is also typical of someone caught up in the contradictions of his life. These contradictions upset him: he knows that he loves his family and doesn't want to hurt them, but can't seem to control himself when he gets home; while at work he is meek and conforming and frightened most of the time.

This Dr Jekyll and Mr Hyde personality is typical of someone who is too nice. Tim's fear in the work environment keeps him in a state of anxiety on the job, while at home he releases his anxiety in totally inappropriate ways so that his family is in fear of him.

We also call this the 'kicking the cat syndrome' because there are many times when people who do not feel capable of voicing their feelings and thoughts in one area of their lives will take it out in another. Tim's work colleagues would be amazed at how aggressively he behaves at home, while his family and friends would be astounded at Tim's anxious posture at work.

For Tim, it really is as though he takes some potion that changes his personality so radically that he could almost not feel responsible for it, certainly not in control of it. His only justification for behaviour that he **knew** wasn't good for him or for anyone else around him was that he truly felt he could do nothing about it.

Please don't shout at me

Louise, like every other person in the world, sometimes gets upset with people she cares about. She's 50 years old, married and works part-time for a small local firm handling their administration. But Louise never lets anyone know she's upset. Or rather, she never lets the person who caused the upset know that she's upset.

What Louise does is tell other people. If she's upset with her husband, she'll tell her best friend. If she's upset with her boss, she'll tell one of her colleagues. If she's upset with her mother, she'll tell her husband. All the people around her are the recipients of her distress except the people who need to hear about it.

Her biggest fear is that if she lets people know she's hurt or angry, they'll shout at her. She's frightened that they'll not only shout at her but that they won't like her for criticising them. So she moves her hurt feelings around a circle of people, none of whom ever know that somewhere along the line they've upset her as well.

Her best friend urges her to talk to her husband, but she says, 'I couldn't do that. He works hard enough all day, he shouldn't have to listen to my silly anger at the end of the day.' Her colleague tells her just to talk to the boss, but she says, 'I couldn't do that. He could find a dozen people like me for this job; it doesn't take a genius and I really can't afford to get fired.'

And so on. Louise's nice behaviour is about fear of triggering other people's anger if she shows them how she feels. We know she's capable of expressing her feelings because she's doing it all the time, just not to the right people. And there are many people like Louise who are wonderful at articulating what is going on for them and how they feel, but feel completely unable to do so face-to-face with the very people who are distressing them. This is a fine example of misdirected emotions which never get resolved so that the storehouse of resentments gets fed continually.

I'm just a guy who can't say 'no'

Jason hides. He hides in plain sight most of the time. He's there, but he hopes against hope that he won't be noticed, especially at work.

Jason is particularly good at certain aspects of his job – he's a regional sales manager for a small firm where he is good at dealing with his customers and his own sales staff. He's affable, understanding, can listen to people's problems with infinite patience and can usually come up with good solutions for them. People like Jason; they think he's a good chap; he will do anything for you.

But Jason never quite lives up to his employers' expectations. They see his easy manner with people and so can't understand why he sits silent as a tomb in meetings; why he never initiates, never offers an idea. They can't understand why, if he can sort out a customer complaint with alacrity, he can't also deal with invoice chasing and uncooperative suppliers. Or why, although his sales staff like him so much, he can't discipline them and his figures aren't as good as those of one of the other regional managers (who isn't nearly as friendly and pally with his staff).

His bosses would like to promote him but feel that there's just something essential missing. They call it drive and ambition, but Jason knows he has plenty of drive and ambition, he just hates to say 'no'. He hates to be the bearer of bad news; he hates to be the bad guy. Most of all he hates the idea that people might think badly of him.

He doesn't realise that although his staff may like him, they also take advantage of his good nature, as do his suppliers: they know he'll never give them a hard time or tell them off.

This form of niceness can be very confusing not only for people like Jason's employers, but for the Jasons of this world themselves. They're doing everything they possibly can to be liked and respected; their bosses see all these qualities and have even hired them for those qualities in the first place! But they also expect some 'backbone' as well and the Jasons just don't have it.

Jason wants to be liked so much that he can't stand to make anyone unhappy. He doesn't realise that a small dose of discipline and clearly defined expectations expressed to his staff and suppliers won't mean he won't be liked. Probably just the opposite: 'he's tough but he's fair' is usually the response about someone who can balance both sides.

In this type of scenario, as in so many others you will read and may very well identify with, the art of saying 'no' is not only absent, it sometimes doesn't even appear on the radar of possible options you might try. Much more on this later.

Wait till your father gets home

Tina and Alan are a 30-something successful couple. Tina is a teacher in an inner-city comprehensive and has no difficulty handling troublesome children. She relishes the challenge her students provide her and comes home, not exhausted, but energised by her action-packed day.

Alan is a civil servant and, contrary to popular belief, doesn't find his job boring in the least. He's employed by a council going through major changes and he likes being part of the planning and arguments, the strike threats and conciliation talks.

At home, Tina and Alan occasionally have explosive rows that never last long, and they enjoy hearing about each other's day and comparing notes about who won which battles. Their political affinity, their sense of humour, a few good friends and love of rambling keep them quite contented.

Most of the time.

Most of the time, except when it comes to parents. This provides them with another common bond as well: they are both intimidated by their parents. They think they love them, but it's hard to tell since their feelings are so mixed up with worrying about what their parents might think.

Christmas is a nightmare. They have to juggle, visiting both sets of parents who both feel that true familial love is manifested by coming for Christmas dinner in the family home. Tina and Alan have never successfully negotiated going to one set on Christmas Day and the other on Boxing Day. Each year they are beset by the same anxiety. And it would never occur to them to have Christmas on their own: they couldn't handle the guilt.

It's not just at Christmas either. They don't answer the phone on the weekends because they don't know how to refuse an invitation to a Saturday party or a Sunday barbecue. They secretly plan their holidays and then spring it on their parents just before they're ready to leave. This way they avoid having to put up with suggestions and hints about being included (which has happened to disastrous effect).

Tina and Alan are typical of the 'wait till your father gets home' kind of nice people. These are successful adults with good jobs, who can face challenges and enjoy productive, fulfilling lives. And yet, when it comes to their parents they revert to acting like frightened four year olds, expecting to be punished, disapproved of, criticised and humiliated if they don't do what their parents want.

For many people, dealing effectively with their parents (or one parent in particular) is often the most difficult thing they ever have to face. They find they just can't do it. All the feelings they experienced as a child come flooding back into their adult selves and render them impotent when confronted by their parents and what they think is expected of them. In some cases it might actually be what their parents really do expect of them, but in many cases it's what they believe is expected. They are so intimidated that they never test it to find out. They never confront or question their parents.

They maintain a destructive status quo that keeps them small and infantile. It can be especially frustrating for people who are strong in their everyday lives. Again, the contradiction will create confusion and anger.

I'm not worthy

A common trait of nice people is that their self-esteem and self-worth is so low they can't really see why anyone would want to be their friend in the first place. Therefore, they feel their only value in any relationship is to provide themselves as a doormat.

They also feel that they always have to be doing things for other people in order to 'earn their keep' in the other person's affections. Take Arthur, for instance.

Arthur has a relatively high-powered job. He's not at the top of the ladder, but certainly higher than the middle. He doesn't really know how he got there since he thinks his skills are negligible. He assumes it must be because he's good at figuring out what other people want and providing it for them. Or it could be that he knows how to use his considerable charm to 'con' people into thinking he has more to offer than he actually does.

He will always take on extra work if he's asked (and even when he isn't), fit in someone else's requests by changing around his own busy schedule, and fill up his days off running errands for friends and relatives.

He knows he gets taken advantage of and he resents it, but he thinks that if he doesn't let himself be pushed around, he won't have any friends at all and certainly won't have his current well-paying job. He feels guilty if he even thinks about saying no. It's a word that hardly ever comes out of his mouth. He is awash with shame if he is ever criticised because he thinks the other person must really see the wormy side of him and be disgusted by it.

He knows there must be a better way to live than this. Every once in a while he does assess his friendships, and it scares him to think that if he didn't act as a doormat, there would be empty spaces where his friends used to be, not just because they wouldn't want to be with him (or so he thinks), but because he might not want to be with them – a much more frightening prospect.

He tends to avoid these moments of introspection because he feels that if he tampers with the delicate structure he has created in his life, the whole thing could come tumbling down.

What he cannot accept no matter how many times he is told, is that people like him for who he is. His friends love his humour, his quirky way of looking at the world, his energy and enthusiasm about current affairs and political issues. His colleagues are relieved that he can handle the difficult clients that everyone else avoids.

Arthur is representative of people who cannot see themselves clearly at all. It's a bit like an anorexic who looks in the mirror and sees a fat person. This kind of nice person looks in the mirror and sees a hopeless, useless, talentless person who has no right to want or need anything. He's happiest being told what he wants.

Seeing the world through nice-tinted spectacles

One of the most bewildering aspects of being stuck in overly nice behaviour is that you may find it difficult, if not impossible, to accept that a great many people don't operate in the world the way you do. In other words, because you may find it 'natural' and 'right' to always put other people first or to tread carefully so that you won't cause an upset or to look at all sides of an argument, you may find it shocking that others aren't doing the same thing. The fact that your life is littered with betrayals, hurts and resentments is a source of great frustration and humiliation.

The reality is that some people don't have the same dialogues in their heads working out what's the right thing to say; some people don't worry about what other people might think about them; some people aren't afraid of offending or causing trouble. There are vast numbers of people who aren't continually editing what they say, who are not concerned about how others might react to their thoughts and feelings; they don't second-guess or assume, or if they do, it doesn't stop them from being clear about what they want. Some people are experts at getting what they want.

You know yourself that there are times when you don't just see the world through nice-tinted spectacles. There are times when you don't edit, second guess or assume the worst. What is important here is for you to identify the times when you do and how they affect you.

When nice people get hurt by something someone did or said to them, they can't always believe that it was done to them in the first place. Such a possibility is so outside their own schematic of the way the world is that they think it must be deliberate. The nice person who resides in this narrow view of the world believes that the other person must know that they're being hurtful, upsetting, dismissive, manipulative, etc. and, therefore, must be doing it just to make them feel bad.

Nice people think that the world **ought** to think the way they do, behave the way they do, feel the way they do, have the same sensibilities as they do. So when the rest of the world doesn't, they suffer. They keep their tinted spectacles on, expecting the world to work the way they'd like it to and setting themselves up to be hurt yet again.

It's simply not true. Not only are there a lot of people out there who aren't nice in the way you are, they don't even know you have a problem, because they're viewing the world from their own perspective and can't see why there's any difficulty in saying what they want when they want it. They don't have a problem, so why should you. They'd probably have just as much difficulty imagining that there is any other way to be than the way they are.

There's an even worse downside for some of you: when these types of upsetting situations keep occurring and you think they're deliberate, then it serves to confirm what an awful person you are after all. You may have highly-tuned antennae twitching, picking up slights and hurts that prove you're worthless and not worthy of consideration.

Here's an example of what we mean:

> Jack is one of a group of eight on the Health and Safety committee for the company where he's employed. Twice a year there is a big review meeting of all the latest directives and updates on Health and Safety issues for the business. The meetings are supposed to be organised during everyone's free time.
>
> However, because Jack and his colleagues are all busy people, finding an agreed date is always difficult. When Jack's in charge of organising a date, he conscientiously phones or emails the other seven to arrive at a mutually convenient time. It takes extra time but he wants to make sure that everyone is happy with the arrangement so he goes out of his way to help people juggle their diaries.
>
> This is done on a rota basis, and when Jack isn't in charge it's a different story. Three of the committee member get together, decide what will work for them and inform everyone else that that's the date and leave it to the rest to sort themselves out for the meeting.
>
> Now, because Jack would never organise a meeting in that way, he can't really believe they've acted like that. It's bewildering. The only reason he can find to explain why

his colleagues are so inconsiderate of his busy schedule must be that they think he isn't worth considering – he's a mere nobody.

Which is the 'right' way to organise everyone's schedule? Jack thinks his is the right way and feels not just aggrieved, but dismissed and unimportant because he wasn't consulted. His colleagues think theirs is the right way. For them, somebody has to take a decision and then everyone else can just get on with it and not make a palaver out of setting a date. It doesn't matter who's right because there isn't a right way.

What is important here is that Jack's perception of the way things ought to be not only creates great distress in him, but it feeds the side of him that believes he isn't worth much anyway. This narrow perspective of how the world is, is a large contributor to damaging self-esteem.

Awareness is all: identifying the contradictions

When you have areas in your life that work well and as you would like, then naturally the contradictions will seem all the more confusing. 'Why am I so assertive at work and helpless with a man?' 'I'm so good at relationships and yet pathetic when I'm with my parents' 'Why do I get on so well with my girlfriend, but at work I spend my time avoiding my boss?'

It is rare to meet someone who has no contradictions, where every area of their life either works brilliantly or where none work at all. There are occasionally people who feel that their entire life is spent as a quivering jelly, but the reality will be different. Unless someone is deeply disturbed and has quite serious psychological difficulties, it is almost impossible to be too nice in all aspects of your life no matter how much you feel that way.

Going back to the assessment earlier in this chapter to identify the contradictions will help put things into perspective for you.

Where do your sensitivities lie? What are the areas where you know that no matter how much you try, you will get caught off guard and exhibit the same behaviour you always do in these situations? What areas of your life would you most like to change? Even the ones that you don't think you'll ever be able to change.

Raising your awareness is the first important step to take in making permanent changes. The more aware you are of what you do, in what circumstances you do it and with whom, then the greater your chances become of changing what you do.

It is vital to notice when you do something so automatically that you only realise it hours, days, even weeks after the fact. These are the times when you have knee-jerk reactions that are so much a part of you that you don't even know you're doing them.

Your first challenge is to bring them from the obscurity of unconscious behaviour up to the point of at least being aware of them as they're happening. A common one for you to practise on is to notice how many times you say 'I'm sorry' when you don't need to.

The next stage to notice is the times when you have a very strong inclination to do something differently and are simply unable to do so. This is one of those times when your head says 'No' and your mouth says 'Yes'. You feel utterly powerless to get the words out of your mouth.

Next are the times you do ask for what you want and may even get it, but feel incredibly guilty and selfish because you asked.

Then there are those occasions when you lose your temper (internally or externally) and seem unable to control what comes out of your mouth. For the purpose of awareness it is important to notice the triggers and what happened earlier in the day or the week that didn't get expressed but got stored up instead.

At this point it isn't necessary to do anything about it: increasing your awareness is such a valuable step because it will give you a clear perspective of what you do and when you do it.

Am I maladjusted, or what?

If you know that your behaviour limits your life, then something will definitely be missing. It could be a sense of fun and of spontaneity. It could be that living in fear is such a heavy burden for you that it feels as though your life isn't moving forward at all. It could be that taking care of others uses up so much of your life that you have almost no time for yourself.

All the while that you have these kinds of limitations in your life, then your feelings of frustration, emptiness and hopelessness will grow.

Then what does it mean to be well-adjusted?

You are well-adjusted when your internal self – your thoughts, feelings, impulses, wants and desires – are in relatively good alignment with your external behaviour. If there is a huge gap between the internal self and the external self, then that alignment is skewed. Becoming better adjusted means that your external behaviour more accurately reflects your internal feelings and desires and that you have these two areas working in tandem more often than not.

Right now it may feel as though you have a whole secret life going on inside, while the outside is operating to a different set of criteria. Your secret world is made up of the conversations you wish you could have, the behaviours you wish you could manifest. It is made up of your shames and embarrassments and guilts. It is made up of all the unexpressed emotions that come from hurts, slights, angers; from yearnings and wants and desires that stay bottled up.

Everyone has a secret life; having one is an important part of being an autonomous person and establishing your sense of 'I'. However, in nice people this 'true self' is often hidden away through fear. This secret self can also be chameleon-like, where you blend in with the surrounding scenery so as not to call attention to yourself. This is when you become what you think other people want you to be and thus your internal and external selves are even farther apart.

It is our hope that the more you get your own 'nice factor' within your own management instead of being at the mercy of your fears and anxieties, then the gap between your internal and external self will narrow and that secret life can come out and play.

2

You Weren't Born Nice

This is just the way I am

However old you are, you've lived with yourself for so long that your behaviour seems a natural part of yourself, like the colour of your eyes or the shape of your hands. It's hard to imagine that you were ever different from the way you are now.

In the main, we're so used to ourselves and our behaviours that we think that this is the way we've always been. We think, 'This is just the way I am.' We may not like it; we may wish we could behave differently when our backs are up against the wall, but we still think we've never really had any other options. We just are.

That's just not true. You aren't just the way you've always been; you are the way you've become. You weren't born 'nice'. When you emerged you knew exactly what you wanted: feed me, change me, hug me, let me sleep. You would do whatever it took to get what you wanted. Sometimes you cried for no good reason other than that you wanted to.

Take a good look at an infant. You may have a child or children of your own, or have infant relatives, or know the infant of a friend. If you've not seen one in the flesh, you'll have seen babies on the TV or in the cinema.

Babies are not nice. They cry when they want something. They're very clear. They may not yet have language, but infants know exactly what they want, and they have no hesitation in letting you know what it is.

Some babies cry a lot and some cry less. Some babies have feisty personalities and some are placid. All babies know what they want and they use their own way of communicating to let the 'caregivers' know. They cry or gurgle or smile or frown. They want to be fed, to have a dry bottom, to be cuddled, to be left alone. They want to sleep or be awake; they want to engage with others or commune with themselves.

They do not think of the consequences of their behaviour. They do not wonder whether their behaviour will offend anyone or upset anyone or make anyone angry. They're not worrying about what other people think; they're not afraid of being criticised or judged. They don't know or care whether their behaviour is inappropriate.

They certainly don't care about making a fuss – that's what they are particularly good at. They're not thinking: 'Should I be doing this?' 'What if it I'm not liked?' When they pop out of the womb infants are utterly self-centred. You, too, once upon a time, were utterly self-centred. And boy, did you ever know how to say no when you didn't like something that was happening, or didn't like that something wasn't happening.

However, during the very necessary socialisation process, another process was taking place as well: you were learning that there were parts of your behaviour that were not acceptable and which, if continued, could mean the withdrawal of love, approval, recognition, etc.

At the same time, you were probably rewarded for being nice, keeping your mouth shut, being compliant, toeing the line. You learned to be extra sensitive to other people's needs so that you could hold on to that love and approval.

'This is just the way I am' somehow endorses the powerlessness that nice people feel whereas, 'This is what I've become' reflects an understanding that this is the way you've been reshaped and therefore you are now in a position to do something about it.

This chapter is devoted to looking at what happened – how you became so nice in the first place. This is a time for you to trace your individual history of adaptive behaviour.

Obviously, every one of you became nice differently and in turn every one of you is nice in a different way. Part of the reason we asked you to define your degree of niceness in Chapter 1 was to help you understand that you are uniquely yourself even if you share a problem that many other people have.

The golden age of parenting

There isn't one, there never has been and if we continue as we are going as a culture there probably will never be one. In each generation, it seems, a few dozen books get written on the 'right' way to rear a child. They often contradict those that were written in the previous generation, and there are television documentaries that tell of the horrific results of parents taking some of these books to heart.

The golden age of parenting is *usually* the parenting we didn't get.

We at Impact Factory are certainly not experts on child-rearing; what we see and what our work is centred around are the results of inadequate and ignorant parenting.

HEALTH WARNING! This chapter is not intended to blame your parents (or any other adults who brought you up) or to imply or infer that they were bad people. Nor do we want you to feel bad about what happened in your childhood.

What we hope is that you will take this opportunity to identify for yourself the source of your current behaviour. Laying blame doesn't help nor does making yourself even more unhappy than you already might be. Knowing how you got this way helps to put the problem into perspective so that you can do something about it.

On very rare occasions there are such people as bad parents. But on the whole it is not bad parents but incompetent parenting that creates nice people. And not even incompetent parenting all the time. We have seen many people who have had loving, caring and very nurturing parents at the best of times. It was at the worst of times, however, that that love and caring turned into irrational, thoughtless and careless behaviour that so adversely affected their children.

Parenting has to be the most difficult job of all time. The responsibility is enormous, the effort prodigious and the task never-ending. Parents are required to have patience beyond comprehension. Yet in most cases there's no training for parenthood. 'It will come naturally' is a glib and useless phrase many women hear in the face of their first pregnancy.

If you are in a job and earning a salary, you most likely received some form of training. People who do voluntary work usually receive training as well. Even if it wasn't as much as you'd have liked, your employers gave you some idea of what was expected of you. Many of you may even have access to top-up or developmental training in your jobs.

When a new disease is discovered (think of the high learning curve doctors, nurses and scientists had to undertake when AIDS first came to the world's attention); when new machinery or a new computer system is installed; when an efficiency study or a reorganisation is implemented – are you left to figure it out by yourself? Unlikely. In most cases where something exists that didn't exist before or something has been upgraded or added, there is training to go with it.

Not so for parents. A health visitor pops in every once in a while. And that's it. If they're lucky (or unlucky depending upon your point of view) they might have a gaggle of relatives and friends to give advice and to help out. But the way our culture is evolving even that is getting increasingly rare.

There are ante- and post-natal classes available and in some more enlightened communities there are short-term seminars on the problems of infant care.

There's almost nothing available to help parents understand all the implications of bringing another human being into the world. They might go out and buy one or two of those few dozen books on good parenting, but since we know they are often contradictory, they may simply confuse the whole process.

So what do they do then? They do the best they can. The best, however, is not always good enough and you are, in adulthood, suffering from the long-term effects of not-good-enough parenting.

So what actually happened?

Not only are most parents inadequately trained to be parents, but children for the most part, are anarchistic monsters and do require a great deal of socialisation in order to become competent members of whatever society they are born into. Children are manipulative, devious, cunning and are for ever testing adults to see just how far they can go. They are self-absorbed and use their clever little minds to figure out how to get their own way, how to get their parents' attention and how to create their lives the way they want them to be. They cannot be allowed free reign or there would be constant chaos.

Each culture, each family, has its preferred way of socialisation and it is necessary for tiny people to learn good social skills in order to get on well in that culture, in that family. This will mean learning to use accepted and recognised forms for communicating needs, wants and ideas; and it will mean learning to use accepted forms of behaviour that both protect you and the society you are part of.

You will have been taught how to eat with a knife and fork; how to use the toilet, how to get dressed by yourself and tie your own shoelaces. You will have been taught manners: not to interrupt when adults are talking; how to say please and thank you; not to talk back; to mind your elders; not to swear, etc. If you had a religious upbringing you will have been taught about a deity and that religion's moral code.

If this isn't done at least to an adequate degree, then we get a climate that makes it possible for children to take that anarchy and impose it – sometimes in brutally criminal ways – on society. We are then back to our analogy of six-foot children in adult guise let loose on the world and completely unable to deal with it.

Now this is where the difficulty lies. Adults have the responsibility of civilising their children, but the process is often anything but civil. In their own frustration and desperation parents will tyrannise, humiliate, bully, criticise, beat, threaten, cajole, scream at, insult, ridicule, emotionally blackmail, tease and in many other ways physically, emotionally or mentally manipulate their children to get them to behave the way they want them to. This kind of manipulation is anything that takes away the dignity of a child or diminishes their self-esteem and self-worth.

We imagine that most of you have encountered a child (usually in a supermarket) whose behaviour was so abominable that you couldn't care less about their dignity; you just wanted them to shut up.

This is where parents get to *after* they get to the ends of their tethers and they have no resources to fall back upon. Most likely they have experienced inadequate parenting themselves and are usually doing exactly what was done to them. Some parents may vow that when they have children of their own, they won't do what their parents did to them. But if they haven't resolved their own sense of inadequacy and learned some new parenting skilled they'll either revert to old habits, or create some brand-new ones.

Now, as well as being anarchistic monsters, children are also delightful, exuberant, spontaneous, creative; full of vitality, mischief, joy and curiosity. They are strong-willed, determined and impulsive. It doesn't take much to curtail, dampen and diminish all that playfulness and spontaneity. It doesn't take much to knock the mischievousness and joy out of a small person.

It also doesn't take much to force a child into the direction the adults would like it to go. They just have to threaten you a few times, scare you out of your wits, give you a good smack or humiliate you, and hey presto! an obedient child.

You make a decision, somewhere along the line, 'I'll never do that again.' It becomes less and less likely that you're going to step out of line for fear of what that misstep might unleash. A steady diet of this doesn't have to be extreme to impinge on the emotional growth of a child; nonetheless, children will be affected by this manipulation to a degree.

One person we know was simply told by his parents over and over again, 'I wouldn't try that, if I were you, you might fail.' These parents loved their child and thought they were looking out for his best interests in helping him to avoid disappointment. But since every time he wanted to try something new he got that message, his sense of self-confidence was whittled down. By the time he reached adulthood he expected to fail every time he went for a new job, started a new venture, made new friends and this sense of failure even imposed itself on his marriage and children.

Bad parents? No – just unskilled.

In our workshops we have heard examples of the full range of parental behaviour, from the horrific and deplorable to the almost comic. For instance:

- A number of children who were beaten every day and locked in closets for hours at a time.
- An adopted child was threatened with being sent back to the orphanage if he didn't behave.
- One girl was told that if her father died (he was ill with a weak heart) then it would be her fault for being noisy.
- One child was left on her own every day and tied with a rope to the back garden fence so she wouldn't wander away.

- Most children have been told that Mummy will leave them in the playground, supermarket, car park, etc if they don't hurry along.
- Families have inflicted the 'silent treatment' on one or more of the children with the resulting farce of a parent addressing the child through another person.
- One person described her father's 'look' which so terrified her that she never needed any follow-up words.
- Children have been told that the bogeyman will get them; that their parents have eyes in the backs of their heads so they can see everything that their child is doing; that Father Christmas is keeping a tally of good and bad deeds and might not come this year unless they shape up.
- Many parents justify certain punishing behaviour by saying, 'We're only doing this for your own good.'

The socialisation, or more appropriately, the manipulation of children's behaviour is for the parents' needs and wants, not for the children's.

We could continue this list for another ten pages but this is the time for remembering some of the things that happened to you, some of the devices that were used to get you to behave. How well do you remember your childhood? Are there some clear memories or are they mostly blurred?

You don't have to have been beaten and stuffed into a cupboard to have been affected by less than nurturing parenting. Unrealistic expectations imposed on a young child will go a long way to fostering feelings of inadequacy and incompetence. You don't have to have heard a harsh or critical word or felt the sting of a smack to adapt your behaviour if you are constantly worried about disappointing your parents.

Repeatedly being told you're not pretty enough, or you'll never excel at sports, or you're clumsy, or you have a funny shaped nose, or you ask too many questions, etc could do it.

For instance, if you were made fun of as a child because you sang off-key or coloured outside the lines, those comments could have made an indelible impression. You may have made a decision never to sing or draw again.

You probably have areas that you're sensitive about now. Chances are they have their roots in things that were said or done to you when you were little. See how specific you can be in pinpointing some of these sources.

If you can't, that's all right, too. Everybody's memory is different: some people remember incidents that happened to them when they were one, while others have only a vague inkling of what might have happened; some others have no memories – their early childhoods are a complete blank. Remember what you can.

It may help to ask a sibling, if you have any, or a close relative who was around at the time, what their memories are of that period in your life. However, siblings are interesting in that they often relate such different childhoods to your own, as though they grew up in a different family.

Even if you can't remember specific incidents from your early childhood, it is generally true that people have very long, good memories for phrases or things that were said to them that were particularly hurtful or embarrassing or humiliating.

> **Robin:** I remember my father was once very angry at some mischief that my brothers and I had got into. I can't remember the incident but I can certainly remember my father's words as clear as day, 'Why was I blessed with such idiots for children!'
>
> Do you think he remembered saying it a day or a week later? Unlikely. But because he said it at a time when I was sensitive, it got right in: it tapped into some deep place inside myself that probably believed I was an idiot or because I so much wanted my father to think of me as clever. Those words have stayed with me ever since. To have disappointed my father with my behaviour was a very shaming thing to have done. It wasn't that I had done something idiotic, it was that I was an idiot.
>
> Making sure no one ever saw me as an idiot became a life goal. I have spent a long time since relearning how to be foolish, make mistakes and to play.
>
> **Jo Ellen:** I remember overhearing my father say about me, 'At least we don't have to worry about Jo Ellen, she can take care of herself.' A throwaway sentence said in the face of one of my siblings being difficult while I was being good (as

usual). Does he remember it as something earth-shattering to me? He didn't even know I'd heard most likely.

But for me it was one of the most crucial things I ever heard said about me. A very little voice inside me was saying, 'No I can't, no I can't.' But I completely ignored that voice because I was so proud to be seen as strong and not a problem which was what I thought was expected of me from then on.

And that's what I've done ever since: taken care of myself, even when, I really wasn't up to it and made a real hash of it as well.

As we said, it doesn't take much to get us to modify our behaviour. A few well-chosen phrases can reinforce beliefs that have been instilled from early childhood and the damage is done, sometimes for a lifetime.

You don't want that

One of the more difficult aspects of nice behaviour is that you sometimes don't really know what you want. You have become so distanced from the feelings and instincts that let you know what you want, that you are completely out of touch with your real desires. This is produced by another aspect of inadequate parenting: your wants may have been denied you.

Take a peek at this scene observed by Jo Ellen a couple of years ago:

Standing at the bus stop is a harassed mother and a little girl of about five all dressed up in a party frock, clutching a Happy Birthday gift-wrapped box. Out of her mouth come the words, 'I don't want to go to Melissa's party. I hate Melissa.'

'No you don't. You love Melissa. She's your best friend. I'm not standing for any argument now, young lady, here's the bus.'

'No she isn't. I hate her and I never want to see her again and I'm not going.'

> 'I don't have time for this, Nat, get on the bus. You always have a good time at Melissa's and that's where you're going!'
> And so ensued one almighty row with Mum yanking Nat onto the bus and Nat screaming blue murder, Mum embarrassed, people looking the other way.

A typical scene of one overworked mother trying to deposit her daughter for a few hours at a party, and here's her daughter creating a scene when she least needs it (they're good at that, children: their radar picks up on when would be the worst time to have a tantrum and then they have it).

This doesn't sound like a bad or mean parent, but the subtle message she was giving Nat was that whatever Nat was feeling wasn't the right way to feel. She was told she loved Melissa, when patently at that point Nat didn't. She was told she always enjoys herself, when just then enjoyment was the last thing on her mind. What is so confusing for the child is that she's being told that what she feels isn't what she feels.

Now it would take tremendous patience at that point to stop the scene, kneel down to Nat's level and say something like: 'What's happened? I thought you loved Melissa. Tell Mummy what the problem is.' In most cases that's pretty much all children need – to be heard and acknowledged. Then some negotiation can go on between the parent and child. She's not being told she isn't feeling what she's feeling.

In the aftermath of a scene like that, Nat may not realise exactly what's wrong, but the denial of her feelings and needs will hit home. And she'll certainly remember the humiliation of being yanked onto the bus and, who knows, may have ended the day throwing up all over Melissa's house in order to express her unresolved feelings.

Another simpler example is one heard around the world. This is our version; you will have experienced or at least heard a similar version at some point in your lives.

> 'I want an ice cream.'
> 'No you don't.'
> 'Yes I do. I want an ice cream.'
> 'No you don't! You don't want an ice cream.'

'I do, I do, I do, I do want an ice cream.'
'I'm telling you, you don't want an ice cream. Now stop
behaving like a spoilt brat and go to your room.'

Like a bad music-hall scene, this one could go on for hours, possibly
ending with a crying or at least sulking child, confused because he knew
he wanted an ice cream and yet was being told he didn't want one. On
the surface it also seems relatively harmless. The parent doesn't want
the child to have an ice cream and that's that.

For us, 'that' isn't so straightforwardly 'that'. Here's what we believe
is a more appropriate version:

'I want an ice cream.'
'I know you want an ice cream, but I don't want you to
have one, it's too close to dinner time.'
'But I want one'
'Yes, I know you want one, but I'm not going to let you
have one right now.'

This too could carry on for a while (children are nothing if not
persistent) and may also end with a sulking child. The difference is that
the child doesn't get confused about what he wants. He may not get
what he wants, but he's at least been given the reasons why without
being made to feel wrong.

If, as a child, you weren't allowed to want what you wanted, it makes
it very difficult to be clear about what your wants are now as an adult.
Can you remember if there were times when you were told you didn't
want something you knew you did? Do you remember how it felt?

Don't be such a crybaby

Along with your being told you didn't want what you knew you wanted,
you may also have been told you weren't feeling what you knew you
were feeling. This so often happens when an adult simply cannot cope
with the tears of a child. A child's tears may awaken the adult's own
unresolved unhappiness, and can make them feel inadequate as a
parent because they can't protect their child from hurt.

In attempting to comfort a child who's crying, these are some of the things an adult might say: 'Don't cry, there's nothing to cry about' or 'Cheer up, it wasn't as bad as all that' or 'Don't make such a fuss.'

If they're trying to get the child to shut up, they might say, 'I'll give you something to cry about' or 'Don't be such a crybaby' or 'Big boys don't cry' or 'Let's show the world how grown up you are.'

None of these demands is particularly helpful, yet all of them undermine the child's feelings. It's very damaging not being allowed to feel what you feel. As with wants, this is very confusing. Again, this is all done for the adult's good, not the child's. It is to relieve the adult from their own uncomfortable feelings.

During the 1996 Olympics there was a scene which typified the kind of denial we're talking about. The person involved was no longer a young child, but it was a perfect example of good intentions getting in the way of true comforting.

It was during the women's gymnastics finals. One of the American gymnasts slipped and fell during her routine, putting her out of contention for the gold medal, or a medal of any kind in that exercise. She left the arena, naturally, in floods of tears – grief, loss, disappointment, embarrassment. Her coach came along to comfort her and as cameras and microphones don't acknowledge that privacy exists, the world was privy to her upset.

This is what her coach said while patting her on the back, 'It's OK, you still have the team medal.' That was a big help. Typical, however, of not letting a person have the feelings that they're having right at that moment.

These are the kinds of unthinking words that parents say when they feel helpless in the face of their child's upset and unhappiness. This is very confusing for the child who is experiencing the feelings. The underlying message is that whatever you're feeling isn't all right.

This is not just confined to situations when a child is in tears. Many parents will criticise a child for being 'over-sensitive' thus dismissing the extent that a child is feeling something. Extremes of emotion can be rather awesome, and many children are made to feel wrong because they express those extremes.

In many families feelings are forbidden: the stiff upper lip is firmly in place and nothing, but nothing, is going to budge it. Try telling that to an infant. Well, some parents do. They are so distressed by what they experience as their child's arbitrary crying and wailing that in their helplessness they will transmit to the child the sense that crying is wrong.

Crying isn't wrong. As we wrote earlier, it is probably the main communication tool that a baby has to indicate its needs and wants. And yet, by a very early age, children (especially boys) are chided for shedding tears, including being told they're doing it on purpose to gain sympathy. Tear ducts were invented for a purpose; and yet to look at some adults and the way they have had their feelings effectively suppressed, you'd think they'd had theirs surgically removed.

Tears are considered to be an embarrassment, a source of shame and a weakness. They are either unmanly or are a manipulative tool used by women to get their own way. Neither sex can win this particular battle if there's a harsh judgement about tears being shed. Either way they are looked on as negative, rather than a means to express the feelings that are going on inside.

What about you? Do you recall any times when your feelings were denied you; when you were told that you ought or ought not to feel a certain way? Were (are) there rules in your family about feelings? Are they encouraged, dismissed, criticised, ridiculed, comforted?

How might this denial of wants and feelings manifest itself in adulthood? If asked what you need or want or how you're feeling, you might answer, 'I don't know'. Most likely, deep down you really do know, but you may be so used to other people defining feelings for you that to bring them from that deep place and articulate them may feel an impossible task.

If you do say what you want, you might be criticised, told you don't want it, not really, and then told what you do want.

Do you find that in your life you have people who tell you what you want? Some people are particularly good at telling others what it is they want – they know. Of course, it's usually what they themselves want, but by making it your want, they push the responsibility onto you. If you've grown up having your wants denied you, it will be very easy to take on someone else's as your own.

Jo Ellen: I watched a mother in a supermarket who had a three-year-old girl in the front of the trolley. She pushed the trolley right up to the biscuit section and said to the little girl, 'Which ones do you want?' I thought, now *that's* the way to do it. The little girl with no hesitation pointed to a stack of packets and said, 'That one.' I waited for the mother to take a box and put it in her trolley. But no; instead she said, 'You don't want that one. You want these, Daddy likes these.' I really had to restrain myself from shouting at her, 'Well, why did you ask her what she wanted in the first place?'

If you get enough of that growing up, as an adult if someone else is insistent about what you want, you'll probably begin to think you do want it after all. Well-meaning people will be starting sentences with 'What you need is…' and you'll believe them and consider what they think you need, which can never be as accurate as what you think you need.

Jo Ellen: One day Robin and I were driving through London, returning to the office. I was driving. There was a fork in the road. I always took the left-hand fork and Robin the right. As we approached the fork Robin said, 'You want to go right', and I dutifully turned right without thinking, while at the same time saying, 'No, I don't.' We fell about laughing at both of our reactions: that's how well ingrained these childhood messages are.

Here are a few other examples we have heard on our workshops.

- One woman's husband (from whom she's separated) keeps telling her she loves him and she keeps wondering if maybe she does because he's so certain.
- Similarly, one man got married when he really didn't think it was a good idea, because his fiancée convinced him that deep down he loved her.
- One man didn't go for a promotion in his firm because a colleague told him he didn't really want the job and so he began to question his own motives.

- One woman kept coming up with holiday ideas she discussed with a friend she was going to travel with and was told she didn't really want to go to any of those places, and ended up going where her friend wanted to go.

Some people find that they literally don't know what they want or how they feel. They find it incredibly difficult to make a decision because they simply aren't sure if what they think they want is really what they want. They are out of practice at identifying their wants and then seeing if it's possible to get them met.

Even more common are people who do know deep down what they want and feel, but are so afraid of the repercussions of expressing their wishes that they'll say: 'I don't know' or 'Anything you want is OK with me' or 'It doesn't matter, I'll go along with whatever' rather than calling attention to themselves by saying 'I want' or 'I feel…'

And what about now? How good are you first, at identifying your wants and feelings and second, voicing them in the hopes of getting them met or acknowledged?

I'm only doing this for your own good

Ever heard that line? It's a lie.

There are many things the adults in our lives did for us that were most definitely for our own good. Each of you will have your own memories of the kind, generous, loyal, playful and nurturing things your parents and other adults did for and with you.

However, our experience is that when you are a child, as soon as an adult tells you something is for your own good it's time to be suspicious. It usually means that it's for their own good, not yours. It usually means that they are trying to get you to adapt and alter your behaviour in order to make *them* comfortable, not to improve your social skills.

When the adults in your life could no longer cope with your antics, it was usually the time when clichés and heavy-duty commands started issuing forth. It was their inability to cope which was really the issue rather than your difficult behaviour. We're not saying that you were necessarily an angel; but it's usually when parents don't know what to do next that children get victimised the worst.

If this kind of thing happened to you, then what may have been particularly confusing for you is that you may have been experiencing life in all its joyous innocence – and then your parents' wrath came like a bolt out of the blue to shatter that innocence and create fear.

And when they started in on you, you began to accommodate your behaviour in order to make it acceptable to other people. This is when you began to develop an extra sense like radar: this is the sense of figuring the right way to behave in order to make everything all right. On a conscious or unconscious level you were on full alert with worries such as: 'What's going to upset my parents?' and 'What should I do now?' and 'What do they expect of me?' and 'How am I supposed to behave?'

If you were very little, then these weren't necessarily thoughts with words; they were more a feeling, an instinct, that you'd better 'shape up' or you could be 'shipped out'. 'Shipped out' in this case might mean the withdrawal of love, affection, approval and acknowledgement – all the reinforcement and reaffirmation that children need in order to feel safe and secure.

When you were young you altered your behaviour to fit in with your parents' (and other adults') needs. Their needs were constantly changing, however, so you had to guess what they were, often unsuccessfully. The ground was unsure and the right to change the rules was in someone else's control. There might even be new sets of rules every day or every week which is really perplexing for little children.

This could mean life was like treading on eggshells for fear of waking sleeping giants, in this case you awakened your parents' anger or displeasure. This meant trying to anticipate potential disasters and dangers by cultivating a heightened awareness of the nuances of atmosphere.

It's as though you developed sophisticated internal radar equipment that picked up the slightest vibration of impending trouble, and then you had to figure out what to do to make sure that trouble didn't erupt. Quite a burden for a young person. You'll have felt responsible for cheering them up when they were down; doing things that would make them happy; treading cautiously so as to avoid notice if they were on the lookout for someone to vent their frustration on.

Robin: A few years ago I overheard my next-door neighbour scream something at his four-year-old son which I thought summed up the terrible but also ridiculous contradiction that children endure at the hands of their parents. This child had obviously done something the father didn't approve of and he shouted at full voice, 'Act your age!'

Well, he was. Four year olds act like four year olds. What the father was really saying was, 'Act the age I want you to be', which obviously wasn't four.

It is these inconsistencies that are particularly confusing. It's as though the goal posts were continually being shifted and you had to be alert enough to notice where they had been shifted to. Failure was inevitable. No young child can be successfully vigilant all the time and you would have most likely displeased your parents at some point no matter how much you tried to avoid doing so.

But practice makes perfect, and you had a lot of opportunities to practise making yourself into someone you weren't. You tried to figure out what was the best, most approved of way you were supposed to behave; and, in a sense, you disfigured yourself in order to transform yourself into this other person.

In the face of all of this, you miraculously survived. Your genuine spirit of courage and hope and the desire to be free of limiting behaviour hasn't been completely squeezed out of you. You devised some simple and some elaborate faculties to cope with the changing rules, shifting goal posts, inconstancies and contradictions you encountered in your childhood.

The way we adapt

In the following section there are descriptions of the most common ways children adapt and alter their natural behaviour in order to win (or not lose) their parents' care. There will probably be more than one that will look familiar to you. They may not be the most helpful behaviours now, but they helped you get through some rough times. They were essential then.

These ways of adapting are some of the personality traits you may have developed as opposed to the ones you were born with. This list includes both personality types and coping and defence mechanisms that you may have created in order to survive. We've separated out some of the specific types of behaviours that nice children adopt and given them names. However, we don't believe that any person is just one of these types but instead is an amalgam of traits, behaviours, quirks and habits, shaped by experience to become the self you now know.

We've delineated these behaviours and coping mechanisms in a form which may help you to look at some of the ways you probably developed as a child. We're using this format more as a model to describe a whole range of possibilities rather than offering it as a clinical analysis.

The idea here isn't for you to read through the list and say 'Aha! I'm a people pleaser and I'm devious.' It's to give you a sense of the kind of behaviours you might have taken refuge in to withstand the stresses of growing up in an environment where the natural, true you was not always acceptable.

So in looking back at how you developed there will be times when you were indeed a Good Caretaker or a Guilty Peacemaker. There may have been times when you withdrew or stayed steeped in shame. Other times you were none of these or all of them all at once.

We also have only listed a few of the behaviours we have witnessed in our workshops. We know there are many more personality types, and you may come up with a few of your own that aren't included.

The good child

Good children are really good. They got the message very early on about how well they were rewarded for doing the right thing: the right thing being whatever it was that their parents wanted them to do. These are the children who rarely complain about extra chores, who don't get their clothes very dirty, who follow whatever the current set of rules is to the letter. They never make a fuss.

These children are also usually invisible: they make themselves that way. The last thing they want is to draw negative attention to themselves. They'll keep very quiet and they may feel as though their lives are being lived in the eye of a storm: it may be quiet on the inside, but all around is danger.

Once labelled a good child, it's almost impossible to shake off the label since it is always expected that they will be good no matter what.

The peacemaker

These children are always trying to keep the peace: they try to settle arguments between parents, between siblings, between parents and siblings. They will smooth things over; they'll eat their greens; they'll be quick to point out all the good features about a TV show, a book, or a person that others have disparaged. They abhor dissension or disagreement.

These children hate arguments of any kind and will go out of their way to avoid conflict or confrontation. They will always say everything is 'fine' when it isn't. They will never let on that life isn't one smooth and pleasant highway.

The obedient child

These children are similar to Good Children, but they tend to live their lives in a great deal of fear. They will be on guard lest they get caught out in some wrongdoing. Even when they haven't been naughty, obedient children expect to be yelled at; they expect to be found out.

They, too, are extremely good at following the rules. So good, in fact, that they make up and follow whole sets of rules of their own about how they are supposed to behave that are often much harsher and more demanding than normal family rules.

The people pleaser

People pleasers are always looking out for the right thing to do or say around the adults. Also known as 'goody two shoes', they can be infuriatingly sweet and they are always looking to score Brownie points by being very clever. They spend much of their time second-guessing so that they can provide whatever might be needed before the adult even knows they want it.

The guilty child

For guilty children, it's always their fault. They assume that whatever is wrong around them, they must be to blame. Thus they find it particularly difficult to have fun, let loose, be rambunctious because of the distress they might cause the adults in their life. They believe that everything they do is going to be wrong or upset someone.

The shamed child

Similar to the Guilty Child, but here it's more about who they are than what they do. Children who feel ashamed of themselves really do believe there is something intrinsically wrong with them. They apologise just for being.

The tattle-tale

These children need to look good by making others look bad. They keep their eyes peeled for others' misdeeds and are prompt to report them to parents and teachers. They also try to score points but usually at someone else's expense.

The caretaker

These children end up looking after their siblings and parents. As a matter of fact, they end up looking after everything, it seems. They make themselves incredibly useful, and parents often rely on these children. They are super-responsible and, as adults, get saddled with more jobs and extra-curricular activities because everyone assumes they love doing them, as they're very good at taking things on.

In America a caretaker is usually called a janitor, and our image of caretakers is of people who are busy mopping up other people's problems and maybe getting a Christmas bonus, if they're lucky.

The self-sufficient child

These are the children who don't need looking after. Of course they do, but they appear so self-sufficient and so capable of handling the difficulties around them, that their parents are usually relieved that there's one less to worry about.

Strong children don't show their vulnerability or their tender sides and are viewed as not being affected by upset in the same way that other, more sensitive, children are.

The passive child

Passivity comes particularly from lying low and not calling attention to yourself. You get so used to letting other people decide for you what you want and how you are supposed to be that it feels impossible to muster the energy and courage to rebel and strike out on your own.

Passive children are incredibly compliant and are able to mould themselves to fit the current requirements, whatever they may be.

Withdrawing

In psychological jargon this is also called 'splitting off' which means just that. For some children the pain of reality is so great that they have to do something to relieve the anxiety and terror. They will do this by quite literally removing a part of themselves from the proceedings. Their bodies may be present and experiencing whatever is happening to them; but mentally and emotionally they will have absented themselves. They go inside themselves to a place where they cannot be touched

We see this most commonly with victims of child sexual or severe physical abuse. However, some children use withdrawing into themselves to cope with parents who continually shout or nag or criticise. For us, the common factor is that whatever is coming from the parents' mouths is pretty much continuous.

If a child is rarely shouted at, then that can be a pretty effective way of getting a child to take notice and behave. But if they are shouted at all the time or continually told what they're doing is wrong, then they will shut down a part of themselves as protection.

They might be smiling and sayings 'Yes, yes, uh-huh, OK, Mum, right' but they're not paying any attention whatsoever. For them it is too hurtful hearing about their deficiencies, and so they don't.

Becoming secretive or devious and lying

All children lie and all children are secretive and devious. It's a natural part of establishing an identity – to have thoughts and ideas and feelings that no one else knows about. It's part of the process of separation, affirming one's own self. If you get away with it, lying is also an effective way to avoid the wrath of parents and teachers, which most children want to do whether they are nice or not.

However, for nice children lying and secrecy take on other dimensions. They become particularly adept at hiding their feelings and thoughts so that no one will know what's going on inside. They learn to mask their feelings effectively so that the world thinks they're OK when in reality they aren't.

They lie and become secretive because they are ashamed of who they are. They are convinced that they have thoughts and feelings that other people don't have and so they hide them away in a very deep place inside themselves to avoid ridicule and shame.

Numbing

Numbing is quite literally that: feelings of any kind are effectively frozen over. They might be there but they've been blocked out. The degree of distress in actually experiencing feelings is so great that children will emotionally anaesthetise themselves rather than suffer it.

Creating an inner-parent

This one's great: after a while the parents don't even have to speak any more. They have so effectively given enough negative messages to their offspring that these children have incorporated their parents' voices inside their heads forever more.

These are the people who, when they do something that they don't think is particularly good, will unleash a stream of criticism at themselves: 'What an idiot you are; you're pathetic. You can't get anything right' and so on. They don't need anyone on the outside to tell them how horrible they are, they're quite adept at doing that themselves.

If you recognise that you have an inner-parent or two, it means you have consumed whole the very tone of voice of the original villain(s) of the piece, except that it sounds just like your voice. Now you can harp on and on all by yourself, at yourself, about your uselessness, your stupidity, your thoughtlessness, etc.

A good way to sum all of this up is to describe the nice child as **an old head on young shoulders**.

Nice children grow up fast. They become adult much younger than is appropriate. But because they have spent so much time observing adults in order to suss out the right thing to do, they take on an adult aura very early on.

They miss out on a lot of their early childhood because they are living in a state of anxiety, concern and apprehension lest they put a foot wrong. They sublimate their needs and wants if they suspect they will displease their parents and they have become so practised at suppressing and denying their natural feelings that they come across as far more mature than they really are.

Believe it or not, you had a choice

As you grew up – each in your own way – you began to adapt your behaviour in order to make the grown-ups around you comfortable. Since you weren't born this way, you became this way through choice.

We can hear you protesting, 'What choice does a two-year-old have? Or a seven-year-old, or a ten-year-old?'

Realistically, the choices appear to be non-existent at that age. We don't think, 'Well now, I have quite a few options at my disposal. I wonder which one I'll choose? I could stand up to my mother and father or I could toe the line.' However ridiculous that might sound, it was still a choice. Some children did not make the same choices that you did; some children in your own family didn't make the same choices you did.

Your choices were governed by fear of severe consequences; by the possible withdrawal of that which made you feel safe. Somewhere along the line you made a decision that in order to avoid being abandoned you would adapt and become someone else.

As these giant gods (our parents, other relatives, teachers, etc) were laying down the law, it didn't feel as though there were many options open to us. There were, it just didn't feel that way.

Here is an exercise which might help you understand what we mean.

Choices exercise No.1

We would like you to go back as far as your memories will take you. Try to remember the first time that you *consciously* altered your behaviour because you realised that would be a wise thing to do in the face of the possible consequences. This was a time when you deliberately changed what you wanted to do and did something else.

Or another version is to remember an early incident which was so shameful or embarrassing or upsetting that it was *after* that that you deliberately altered your behaviour so that you would never have to go through that again.

This could have been an argument you overheard between your parents that you thought was your fault and so you tried hard not to 'trigger' their quarrelling by anything you said; it could be a time when you were humiliated at school in front of your class; it could be when you were singled out by an adult for 'naughty' behaviour that was really just play.

However young you were, you were able to observe the situation and consider the consequences of any number of actions you could take. And then you consciously took one course of action over another. Your mind was capable of comprehending the probable results if you did one thing over another and you made a *choice* that would be the best thing to do: you picked the lesser of two evils.

For many of you, although there was actually a choice, it felt like no choice. The consequences of not adapting were so frightening that it felt as though you had no real option.

When choice becomes habit

As a child you were confronted with having to make these choices on a constant basis. Every day of every week of every month there would have been a new challenge for you to face, consider and make a choice about your behaviour.

You will have figured out which were the safest and most appropriate choices for you and after a while it didn't even feel as though you were making conscious choices at all. After a while you will have become so used to altering and accommodating your behaviour that it really seemed as if this was who you really were.

Back at the beginning of the chapter we used the phrase: 'This is just the way I am.' You became so practised at developing choice into habit that it seems that way.

The human being is a pattern-making mechanism. That's good. We don't have to continually relearn how to do things each time we undertake a task. Part of our brain thrives on repetition. We learn through rote.

As we said earlier, it's quite easy to get children to behave by terrorising, humiliating, threatening, bullying them, etc. A child continuously exposed to any one of these tactics will learn quickly how to shape their behaviour so that it doesn't happen any more. Having learnt through rote we develop habit through rote as well.

There are some lessons we absolutely must learn in order to physically survive our childhoods. Here's an example of what we mean:

The Green Cross Code

Every culture that has traffic and traffic lights will have a way of teaching little children to cross the street. Why? Because children do not understand traffic; they do not have a concept of injury the way adults do; they do not understand distance and speed. Parents and teachers do and so to take care of their own concerns about their children's safety, a form of the Green Cross Code is taught.

In Britain it's, 'At the kerb look right, look left, look right again. If it's all clear, quick march, don't run.' This is a very useful set of rules and it's drummed into little heads over and over until they learn it. And from then on, that lesson will govern the choice they make when crossing the street.

You'll have learned your version of the Green Cross Code to help you cross the street safely. And you will have followed it.

Until you got older. Until you began to understand traffic and understand the risks involved if you jay-walked or ran instead of quick marched. Then you began to see that there were other choices. You didn't always have to follow the rules once you realised when they were no longer appropriate. You broke a habit.

However, emotional habits are much harder to break. You may be able to say to yourself as you see a car coming in your direction, 'It's not going that fast; I'll just zip across the street before it gets to me,' and successfully negotiate a quick dash to the other side. But it's not quite that easy when what you're dealing with isn't external traffic but internal emotional pressure. This is a completely different kind of choice than the ones you have been so used to making most of your life.

Choices exercise No. 2

Think of the most recent occasion when you *consciously* knew you wanted to do one thing and ended up choosing to do something different. What happened? Did you even voice an alternative choice? Were you talked out of it? Did you talk yourself out of it?

In the end how did you actually make the choice that you did? Now go back to Choices exercise No. 1 when you first made a conscious choice as a child. Are there any similarities? Were any of the feelings the same? And most importantly, did it feel as though you had no real choice after all? Regaining your choice is ultimately what *The Nice Factor* is all about.

In the next chapter we describe why emotional patterns and habits are so very difficult to break.

3

Whose Reality Is It Anyway?

Have the punishment fit the crime

Jo Ellen:
A number of months after Robin and I created The Nice Factor workshop, I was driving in the country with a friend. It was blackberry time and as we passed lush hedges growing everywhere covered in plump berries, she suggested we stop to pick some.

We were on a narrow country lane without a house in sight. It was peaceful, the late summer sun was shining benignly. And there we were, picking, eating and chatting away.

Then a car pulled up. Instantly everything in me froze. My heart sank and speeded up at the same time; my throat tightened, my knees went weak and I waited for an enraged property owner to start telling us off. I braced myself.

Actually, the people were lost and wanted directions.

I was left with an extraordinary sense of relief mixed with a desire to get back in the car and make tracks before the real blackberry owners came along and told us off.

Now the interesting thing here is that we are talking about blackberries. We are not talking about creeping onto someone's property in the dark of the night with a metal detector searching for ancient artefacts. We are not talking about the Crown Jewels or someone's precious Rembrandt. We are talking about £3.50 a punnet at Waitrose. Besides, everybody picks blackberries whenever they get the opportunity!

Yet I had a physical and emotional reaction as though I had been caught committing an awful crime. My emotions were hugely out of proportion to the situation and at the same time my logical self went walkabout. Even if those people were the landowners and even if they were angry that we were picking their blackberries, my internal reactions were far greater than this particular wrongdoing required.

Acting a little shamefaced; proffering a few apologies; giggling at being naughty children: those reactions might have been appropriate. But I was entangled in a welter of emotions that had nothing to do with the reality of the situation.

Dire consequences

This is one of the key points about the crippling effects of over-nice behaviour.

Fear of consequences is one of the most troublesome issues that you will have to deal with if you want to change your life. Whether the potential consequences really are as dire as you believe (and sometimes they are) it is your belief that they *always will be* that keeps you from trying.

Nice people react to things to a far greater extent than is justified for most situations. This is when our heads say 'no' and our mouths say 'yes'. This is why we can have long conversations in our heads, think of brilliant retorts and devastating arguments and find ourselves unable to utter a word.

While our minds are racing with clever things to say, or when we're having an angry reaction to what someone may be saying to us or when we want to shout, 'That's not fair!', our emotions go to their battle stations and take charge of our brains. We lose the capacity to say the things we want to say.

Instead, we become paralysed, or we dither or say the complete opposite of what was in our heads. We begin to imagine the worst possible consequences if we said even a tenth of what we were thinking: we'd be sacked from our job; our husband/wife/lover would leave us;

our mother/father/gran/etc would never forgive us; our best friend would never talk to us again.

We imagine offending or hurting other people's feelings. We imagine that other people will think we are stupid, thoughtless, naive, uncaring, heartless, self-serving or pathetic. We imagine that other people will disapprove of us; they'll ridicule us or poke fun; they'll be displeased. Because we live in dread and expect the worst, we will do anything to prevent that from happening, including, and especially, not saying what needs to be said.

What happens is a kind of emotional unreality. Imagining an irate blackberry bush owner is going to come leaping out of his car brandishing a shotgun is not being in touch with reality. Having such a reaction in the first place severely limits our ability to see the situation clearly. Excessive feelings get in the way of a rational approach to what is happening.

We cannot respond effectively and with spontaneity because of what we imagine the outcome will be. Fear of the consequences keeps us stuck. We feel unable to change an uncomfortable situation because we have already anticipated that terrible things will occur if we dare to say what we think or feel.

Now it's very possible that as you're reading this you're saying, 'Ah, but it could happen.' You may even be able to cite an instance (or two or three) when you did get sacked or your boy/girlfriend left you or your favourite aunt put down the phone on you. You may remember a time when saying what you thought triggered a rage in someone else or caused them to burst into unceasing tears.

Yes, you're quite right. It could happen. Sometimes terrible things do happen. Sometimes the worst possible scenario is played out with us in the central role. Sometimes we are yelled at, humiliated, disapproved of, made to feel wrong. Sometimes we are abandoned, rejected, overlooked for promotion, talked about behind our backs, made to feel two inches high. However, nice people live their lives as though *every* time is a time when the worst possible consequences will occur.

Remember the sophisticated radar equipment we mentioned in the last chapter? How you probably developed a version of it so that you could be on the lookout for danger zones when you were growing up? Well that equipment is still in operation today.

This creates a kind of super-guarded state of wariness: being on full alert to spot potential disaster. It means being in a constant state of readiness in case something *might* occur that could cause humiliation, embarrassment, upset or hurt. It means second-guessing what might happen and thinking through all the possibilities, all the angles, all the ramifications.

All this seems normal to the nice person: this is just the way I am. This narrows down the possibilities in your life; it limits the choices you have because you've already decided on the outcome. If you tend to operate from a place of anticipating impending disaster, you'll tie yourself up in knots of worry and over-concern.

This anticipation of the worst kills your spontaneity. It shuts down your impulses and knocks your instincts off-centre. To make matters worse, the less spontaneous you are, the less you are able to deal with dire consequences when they do, on occasion, occur. While you are spending time worrying about what might happen and being on guard lest you are taken unawares, your capacity to respond naturally to difficult situations is undermined. It's as though your emotional resources shrink every time you react with fear and apprehension.

It seems a contradiction, on one level. If you are well guarded then it seems logical that your experience will alert you to danger so that you can act effectively. Not so, unfortunately.

All your experience does is trigger well-worn emotional reactions that simply repeat themselves in the new situation. Thus, the fear of the blackberry-owner isn't about being caught red-handed (or blackberry stain-handed) but rather a strong echo or repetition of countless humiliations suffered in the past. That's what makes having a natural reaction so difficult. If your automatic response comes out of your worst past experiences, you cannot judge the current one with clarity.

Sometimes we think that we can be prepared for every potential emotional difficulty that we could encounter. We can't. To think so takes the focus away from what options we have when we are in such situations and puts it on what we fantasise is the right thing to do.

Patricia's story illustrates another aspect of how early traumas and difficulties can revisit, impose themselves and blight the present.

Patricia is a personal trainer and works freelance; she relies on being paid on a regular basis by her clients. This is where her personal 'nice factor' came into play and made her life impossible at times. She simply couldn't ask her clients to pay her on time. Not only that, if they were late for appointments she would work the extra time to give them the full hour and then not charge them for the extra time.

Patricia became overly nice as a young girl when her experience of authority figures was particularly scary for her. She was a little girl sent away to boarding school at three. She associated all grown-ups with raised voices, possible punishment and disapproval. So she adapted her behaviour to be a good little girl so she wouldn't get into trouble.

The real trouble is that the fear which was reasonable then lasted into adulthood. In most cases it wasn't particularly serious, even if it did dampen her quite high spirits. But it was on the work front that the problems arose.

From the outside it was easy for friends and other colleagues to say, 'What exactly is the problem? Just ask them for the money. It's not as though you haven't earned it.' From inside Patricia's life, the idea of asking for payment earned was as difficult for her as breaking all the rules she had grown up with. She was dealing with her clients as the old authority figures who were so scary to her.

Patricia's feelings were very real to her. She needed to be able to deal with the feelings of fear as separate from her clients. Her clients weren't out to terrorise her. Perhaps they were a little slow in paying because she never demanded it from them; and certainly the more often she didn't charge for extra time or leave on the dot of an hour, the more they would take advantage of her. But they weren't monsters.

Fearing consequences is only half the equation that keeps our spontaneity at bay. Here is the second half.

Making it up and acting as though it's true

To a certain extent everyone makes up things in their heads and then believes that they are the truth. Somewhere along the line we get the wrong end of the stick and make an assumption about what someone else is thinking and we convince ourselves so completely that it is true that we make decisions based on that assumption.

However, too nice people do this chronically. They will assess a situation based on their fear of consequences and then adapt their behaviour to what they have decided is the truth. Here is a typical situation:

Emma is approximately 40 years old and an only child of parents who are in their mid-70s. She lives alone in London but within easy commuting distance to her parents in the suburbs. She spends at least two Sundays a month with them. She enjoys their company and spending this time with them. She also has lots of other interests and friends.

Every year Margaret and Ted, good friends of Emma's who live in the country, invite her to spend Christmas with them. They have a large and boisterous family who all get on with Emma and enjoy her company very much.

Every year Emma declines, saying she couldn't possibly upset her parents by not spending Christmas with them; how much they love making a fuss over the Christmas lunch and all the presents and ritual. Margaret has tried every argument: one year won't make that much of a difference; Emma can always spend Christmas Eve with them and make it extra special; her parents have each other; why not just ask them how they'll feel,

But no, Emma counters with her own arguments: they're getting old; it might be their last Christmas; they rely on her to be there.

One year, Margaret and family stepped up the pressure and insisted she came. They humorously told her the friendship would be in jeopardy if she didn't turn up.

Poor Emma. She felt boxed in: on one side were her friends, where she really wanted to go, and on the other, was her own sureness about her parents' disappointment if she didn't spend the day with them. She spent hours on the phone with Margaret and other friends talking about how upset all this was making her. She went over all the arguments and justifications countless times, till all her friends were driven crazy by her indecision.

Everyone said, just ask your parents and find out how they feel. 'I couldn't do that. Then they'd know I don't want to be with them at Christmas and it would make it even worse.'

Finally, Emma gave in to all the pressure and one Sunday, a month before Christmas, with heart pounding and knees trembling, she casually asked her parents how they'd feel if perhaps, maybe, she wasn't really sure, but it was a vague possibility she might be invited to spend Christmas away from London, but nothing was definite. And of course if they were really upset, she wouldn't dream of going.

Her parents' reaction? 'We always wondered why a young girl like you wanted to spend every Christmas with us – you should have done this years ago. We're always pleased to see you of course, but we always thought you didn't have anywhere else to go.'

How many years had Emma stopped herself from doing what she wanted to do because she believed her parents would be devastated if she didn't show up for Christmas? She made up in her head what she thought their reactions would be and made her decisions based on what she had made up.

Emma had limited her choices because she had convinced herself that her thoughts were the truth; and without ever asking her parents how they felt and thought about the situation.

Here's another example.

Geoff, a young salesman, is very keen and ambitious. That's why the electrical goods shop where he works hired him in the first place. They like his enthusiasm and the way he gets on with customers.

Geoff, however, is quite intimidated by people he sees as better and smarter than he is; someone like his boss, for instance. He wants to get ahead and he believes the only way he'll be able to do that is to please his boss and not put a foot wrong. Thus, when his boss, Mr Fraser, came to him during his second week and asked if he could stay late to help with the inventory, Geoff said he'd be glad to stay, he didn't have anything else to do anyway.

The next week he was asked if he could stay late to help with the receipts. He said the same thing – and a pattern was set. Usually once a week, but sometimes more, Geoff's boss would ask if he could stay late, and every single time Geoff said yes. Geoff's friends asked if he was being paid overtime and he said it never occurred to him to ask for overtime – it was just part of his job. They, of course, didn't agree.

The first real clash came when he had to cancel an arrangement he'd made with a couple of his mates to meet in a pub. He figured that as he saw them all the time, missing one night wouldn't hurt. The next clash came when a friend asked him to play in the snooker doubles rounds at their local club. Geoff said he couldn't risk making the commitment because he didn't know which nights he might be asked to stay.

As this went on Geoff began to notice that his friends didn't invite him out as much. When he asked them why, they said they didn't bother any more because he usually backed out at the last minute when he had to work late.

Things really got bad when Geoff started going out with his first serious girlfriend. At first she liked his ambition and didn't mind him rearranging their times together because she wanted him to do well. But after a while, she began to think something wasn't quite right.

'You've been doing this for six months and not getting paid? That's just plain stupid. At least ask for a raise or a promotion or something.'

'I couldn't do that. If Mr Fraser wanted to give me a raise he would have done it by now. No, he expects me to be there and if I'm not, there are a lot of other lads just as good as me waiting to take my place.'

'Don't be ridiculous! You could just ask him; he's not going to fire you just for asking, you know.'

'No, but then he'll think I'm not really all that keen. Besides, I don't think he really likes me all that much anyway; he hardly ever talks to me and he looks angry when I'm around.'

Geoff not only knows what his boss is thinking, he also knows what his boss is going to do. In reality, he's made all this up. How can he know? He's never spoken to Mr Fraser about it, he's never voiced his concerns about working late for no pay.

He's operating in a state of super-guardedness, he's already figured out the worst possible consequences and he's assumed what his boss is thinking about him and how he feels about him, and all his behaviour on the job is based on those assumptions. He does unpaid overtime because he thinks it's expected of him; and what's more, he thinks that if he asks to be paid, he might actually get sacked. He's assumed his boss doesn't like him and he is frightened to do anything about it.

By operating out of his fear, it never occurs to Geoff that his boss is simply delighted he's got an employee who is so enthusiastic about learning the business. He's a canny businessman and chooses to ignore the fact that he's getting a lot of free labour, but he figures he won't do anything till Geoff asks and he'll probably give him a good bonus at Christmas anyway. In fact, he likes Geoff and intends to develop him long-term. He has no idea that Geoff thinks he doesn't like him. Whereas Geoff thinks he looks angry, Mr Fraser's other colleagues know, he's simply preoccupied most of the time.

It wasn't until after Geoff did one of our workshops that he developed a way to talk to Mr Fraser and found out that everything he had been thinking was untrue. If he had stayed much longer without discovering the truth he would probably have found a reason to leave this very promising job. He would never have known that anything was different from the way he had it figured in his head.

Second-guessing, making assumptions and then adapting your behaviour on no other evidence than the scenario you've created in your own brain is dangerous.

Another way to look at this is by seeing it as 'double-think' which means not only having your own thoughts but having the other person's as well. You have your thoughts, then their thoughts about your thoughts. Then you have your feelings about their thoughts and so on. Hard work.

It gets complicated when you look at it this way, doesn't it? Your mind is not only chattering away, reflecting your point of view of the current situation, but it's also having a conversation with you about someone else's view based on your fears, rather than reality.

If we couple this double-think with fear of dire consequences, it's no wonder we tie ourselves up in knots of anxiety and distress. We unfortunate nice people don't stand a chance: our minds are continually sabotaging us.

All of this reflects the ideas in the last chapter. You had a lot of practice at second-guessing what you thought your parents/teachers/etc wanted and you've carried that over into adulthood to such a degree that you're now limiting the choices that are available to you.

Having described the thought gymnastics your mind plays when confronted with stressful situations, let's now look at what happens with your feelings.

Identifying your feelings

As we saw in Chapter 2, everyone becomes nice in his or her own unique way. So, too, each of you reacts to situations in your own unique way. You may identify with some of the case studies we have included, but your feelings are yours and your behaviour is yours.

Therefore, we have devoted this part of the chapter to help you identify some of the feelings, thoughts and physical reactions that you have when you find yourself being too nice for your own good. Here are two small exercises you can do that will help you to identify what happens to you in these situations.

Nice/nasty exercise No. 1

Before you even begin, did you have a reaction to the title of the exercise? Just note it for the moment.

You can do this exercise on your own or while you are with other people, whether you know them or not, since everything is going to take place in your head. If you are alone, imagine you are sitting between two people. They can be anybody – people you know or people you just make up. If you are on a bus or the underground or in an office, note the people sitting or standing on either side of you. The idea is that you have in your mind two different people, one on each side of you.

Whether you are alone or in public, you are now to think of something nice to say to the person on your right; in other words, pay them a compliment, and imagine saying it out loud directly to them. Notice how you feel. Was it easy to find something complimentary to say? Did you think of something and then discard it because you thought it wasn't complimentary enough or that if you said it out loud they wouldn't believe you anyway? Was it a pleasant feeling or were you embarrassed? If you have the opportunity, write down some of the feelings you experienced.

Notice if you had any physical reactions. Did your heart speed up or did you notice that you were smiling as you thought of something nice to say? Did you have a warm, glowing feeling or did you want to get it over with as soon as possible?

Next, imagine the person on your left and think of something nasty to say to them, or in other words, insult them. Imagine saying it out loud directly to them. Notice what happens to you this time. Did you giggle? Did you think of quite a few things and discard them because you couldn't possibly say anything like that to them? Did you think, 'What a stupid exercise. Now they want me to become a nasty person and say insulting things to people?' Did you think, 'I could never say anything like that to anyone, what's the point?' Did you think, 'I can't think of anything nasty to say to someone I don't even know?' or 'I can't say something nasty to someone I know?' Could you think of lots of nasty things, 'because this is just a game, so I won't really have to say them'?

Again, if you are able, write down what happened to you. Did your stomach tighten? Did you have a smile on your face while you were imagining saying something nasty to the other person? Did you just want to say nothing at all? Perhaps you even went away on a little mental journey rather than do the exercise. Did your throat close and did you mentally wince at what was being asked of you? Did you relish the idea of being able to say something mean and horrible?

Did you make up a long list of excuses why you shouldn't do the exercise? Were you editing furiously what was all right to say and what wasn't; what might offend the person and what might be safe?

And were you imagining what their reactions to you might be? Did you imagine the other person getting angry, hurt, upset, outraged? Did you imagine they might attack you verbally or even physically? Did you imagine that they would be shocked or deeply insulted? Write down as many reactions, physical, emotional and mental that you can remember.

Nice/nasty exercise No. 2

Bring into your mind the last time someone did something or said something to you that hurt or upset you; that made you angry or unhappy and you didn't do anything about it. You either accepted it or felt maybe it was your fault anyway or that maybe they had a point. Perhaps you simply felt unable to do anything at all.

Remember exactly where you were, what you and the other person were wearing, if there were any other people present, where you were physically, what time of day or night it was. In your head you are recreating as much as possible the last time you were so nice that you didn't manage to say what was on your mind.

Now remember the feelings you had as you were once again behaving differently from the way you wanted to. These are the feelings you had when you knew what you wanted to say and couldn't. These are the feelings that welled up as all your good intentions about sticking up for yourself ebbed away. These may even be feelings you didn't experience until minutes, hours, days after the actual incident.

Did your heart rate increase, did your throat tighten and your stomach have butterflies? Were you smiling outside while hurting inside? Did you giggle and shuffle around? Did you say something completely inane? Did you blank out for a while and not fully take in what was happening? Did you think it was all right for them to behave as they were doing and that somehow you must be at fault? Did you shrink and look at the ground?

Was this one of those situations where you made up what you thought the other person was thinking and then acted as though it were true? Did you assume what the other person's response was going to be if you did say what you really wanted to say? If you are able, write down all the feelings you had at the time. Did you feel depressed, put-upon, disarmed, out-manoeuvred?

Now go back to that scene and imagine saying everything that you wanted to say at the time. You may experience relief or delight at getting it all off your chest, but are there any other feelings? Did you find yourself saying, 'I could never do that?' What do you imagine the reactions of the other person would be if you did give an airing to all that was on your mind?

Having identified for yourself what happened to you, compare this list to the one where you had to imagine saying something nasty to someone. Are there any similarities? Were your reactions close to or identical in each situation? Were they completely different?

What happens to you?

Even doing these exercises in your head will produce some kind of reaction. We are governed by a whole host of feelings that, at times, seem to be in control of us instead of the other way around. Our logical minds will usually know exactly what to do to protect us and take care of us, while our emotional selves will crumple in a heap. Our emotional sides often have the upper hand, seemingly against our will.

It is essential for you to identify what happens to you when you are in a situation where you don't know what to do, or feel unable to do what you would like. Not what you think *should* happen to you, or what you wish *would* happen to you, but what actually *does* happen to you.

We also don't want you to become a nasty person or to learn to be able to say nasty things. Then you'd just be the opposite of what you are now. These two exercises have been designed only to help you identify your physical and emotional responses to difficult situations.

If even the *thought* of having to say something nasty creates uncomfortable feelings in you, then that is a clear indicator of the powerful long-term effects of being too nice: it's not just the actual situations that distress you; simply thinking about them can cause distress.

You can't do anything to change your behaviour until you know what that behaviour is. All the physical, emotional and thought responses are indicators of what you do. Tracking and noticing your behaviour will help get you conscious which is the vital first step to making effective changes.

These are some of the ways people behave that we have observed when we have done similar exercises on our workshops. See if any of them are similar to what you do:

> Smiling • giggling • wanting to cry • clasping your hands • shuffling your feet • avoiding eye contact • perspiring • blushing • stammering • going blank (not being able to think of what to say) • feeling feverish • shaking • fidgeting • laughing nervously • covering your mouth • having a dry mouth • biting your fingernails • feeling faint • talking a lot • shaking your head • staring at the floor • sighing • hesitating •

We see time and time again people who simply don't realise that they are grinning when someone is bullying them; or that they fidget and stammer when they're trying to get their point of view across; or that they avoid eye contact and chew their fingernails when someone is criticising them. Their physical reactions reflect their inner agitation.

They also do something else: these physical indicators give signals to other people that you are uncomfortable. No matter how much you may think you are masking that inner agitation, your body language will say something different.

Let's say that one of your colleagues at work teases you all the time by calling you 'fatty'. It appears to be done good-naturedly, so at first you go along with it because you don't want to appear over-sensitive. But, eventually, you've had enough and you decide you just have to let that person know you don't like it.

So you say, 'I really don't like it when you call me fatty; I wish you'd stop.' The words are good and you think you've done the job. But the problem is that while you were saying those well-thought-out words you were smiling. If the smile is automatic it means that you aren't even aware it's there. This is you exhibiting one type of behaviour unconsciously while thinking you are doing just the opposite.

The words on the one hand and the smile on the other give a mixed message which the other person can interpret as a kind of licence not to take your request seriously. This can be even more frustrating than the original hurt. There you are, having worked up the courage to confront someone and tell them what you think, and they don't listen. It's as though you'd actually said to them, 'It's all right; I don't really mind if you call me fatty.'

If they continue to tease you, then you can use it as a perfect excuse as to why it doesn't work to tell people what you feel. They don't take you seriously, anyway, so why bother. It will also be confirmation that dire consequences are lurking, waiting to happen when you stick your neck out.

It is unlikely that you will be able to change your behaviour at the snap of your fingers. We're not asking you to. What we are asking you to do through these exercises is to raise your awareness, to get you to notice the things that you do that may indeed give contradictory signals to other people.

Fight or flight or just not there?
Fight

As we have said, your emotions create a lot of reactions in your body. Whether you are happy, sad, frightened, angry, your body will react in your unique way. In particularly stressful situations your body goes into 'fight or flight' mode in order to prepare you to defend yourself.

On occasion you may choose to fight: you may decide to stand up for yourself, say what's on your mind, throw caution to the wind and tell the other person what you think. Stress hormones are released into your body, your heart will beat faster, your breathing may become rapid: these are all good body indicators that you are preparing for a fight.

There may be many situations which occur in your daily life where you don't spend one nano-second worrying about the consequences or whether you'll upset someone. Some people go into fight mode if they feel their children are being threatened; some if they see an injustice they feel strongly about; some if their property is being abused; some if they have a cause that's close to their heart. In these instances, the body preparation for a fight of some kind works to your advantage because no matter how nice you are, your need to 'put things right' will be stronger than your fear.

Fight, however, as a useful tool to make your life more bearable, is rarely considered as an option. It's one thing to defend your child, it's quite another to defend yourself when someone is taking advantage of you during a business meeting, or taking the best room on a shared holiday, or assuming that you'll do the school-run again, even though you were planning to do something else that morning.

Flight

On other occasions you will choose flight: you will back down, give in, avoid conflict, physically leave the situation. These are the situations where you put your needs and wants to one side and let others get theirs met.

How can giving in mean flight? What you are really fleeing is the possibility of confrontation if you stood your ground and decided to fight. Saying, 'No, I can't do the school-run today; it's not my turn, you'll have to find somebody else' may create a confrontation. If you've already made it up in your head that saying something like that will cause an upset in the other person, it feels easier to use the flight option than the fight one.

This type of flight means that you're still living with the difficulty; it never goes away. The school-run will be there yet again on another day. When it's inconvenient for someone else, you'll be the first port of call.

Flight can also mean walking out of a relationship, quitting a job, ending a friendship, all without letting the other person/people know how you feel (or, if you do let them know how you feel, it's usually done in such an explosive, close-ended way that there's no room for discussion). In these instances you may justify to yourself all the good reasons why you've walked out. But you leave carrying all the hurt or anger with you, leaving the other person bewildered and confused because they didn't know there was a problem in the first place – or, if they did know there was a problem, didn't know it was that bad.

In both types of flight, once again, stress hormones are released into your bloodstream, your heart rate will increase and your breathing become rapid. But instead of using all that energy to help you do battle, you suppress it. The excess energy might help you get out of the door but suppressing it does nothing to resolve the difficulty. Indeed, you may use that excess energy to continue to feed the pain, by going over and over in your head what happened, what you could have done or should have done, how awful the other person is and how awful you feel.

Now, flight is a very good option sometimes. If you're being abused, if you're in a situation where staying and arguing isn't going to get you anywhere; if you need to give yourself time to think, then get out! Flee. Run away.

But flight not followed by careful thought and choice will simply perpetuate the problem, not make it any better. It may be that the relationship does need ending, the job needs quitting, the friendship needs terminating, but we know that overly nice people will become habituated to avoiding conflict by 'bridge burning'.

We use the term 'habituated' because once someone finds that they can simply walk away from an upsetting situation without having to confront it, this tends to become the most used option.

Some nice people will leave a trail of quit jobs, broken relationships, and badly ended friendships; they will move house, town, even countries, because they don't have any practice in using any other option.

Beam me up, Scotty

As well as fight or flight, however, there is a third reaction. One of the things that sometimes happens to people under stress is a form of unconsciousness. We don't mean faint dead away; rather you may simply vacate the premises. Your body may be present, the lights may appear to be on, but there's no one at home!

Your desire to be anywhere else but in the present circumstances will cause you to stop paying attention to what is happening around you. We call this going into a 'trance state'.

It's not a literal trance, but the result is the same: the part of you that deals with feelings is put on hold until the current situation is over. You endure rather than confront or run away. It's a way of protecting yourself from unpleasantness. You switch off and withdraw inside yourself so that you don't have to acknowledge just how badly you feel.

In the last chapter we described 'splitting off'. In certain situations you split a part of yourself away from the uncomfortableness of the moment. It's as though the present is so unbearable that you know you have to get away from it and yet at the same time you feel completely paralysed. Staying present physically while being somewhere else emotionally and mentally is a way to disengage from the process and yet not appear to be disagreeing or disagreeable.

We first learn to do this when we're quite young, not just to block out things that are unpleasant but also to block out things we don't want to hear. How many of you can remember selective deafness when a parent told you to clean up your room or do your homework? That's a very benign form of vacating the premises.

However, the less benign forms of splitting off happen when there is emotional or physical abuse and you do not yet have the resources to deal with it. The added difficulty with this defence mechanism is that it cannot discern a genuine threat from one which is triggered by your own irrational thought patterns.

As a little boy, Edward was continually criticised by his parents. He could never quite come up to the standards of his older brother, and they frequently pointed out his deficiencies. Since they didn't expect any answers from him except a promise that he'd try harder, he discovered that he could look at them as though he was listening to what they were saying and go off on a little journey of his own inside his head. Sometimes he fantasised that a wondrous and horrible monster would come along and gobble them up right in front of his eyes. But most of the time he just thought about something else. When they stopped their harping he would bring himself back, promise to do better and that would be that.

Now as an adult, if he senses the slightest whiff of criticism, he's off on one of his mental journeys. It doesn't matter who it is, his MD, his wife, even his children, if someone says something that could be vaguely construed as telling him he's not up to scratch, then he disappears inside himself. He doesn't even know he's withdrawing but other people do. His wife and children are constantly saying, 'You're not listening', but since that too sounds like a criticism to him, he doesn't really hear that either. Or if he does decide to respond, he just repeats back parrot-fashion what they've just said.

Edward is in a double-bind because he's exhibiting behaviour that other people can see, but he can't.

Going into a trance state as Edward does provides you with a way to avoid feeling attacked when someone is giving you a hard time. But it also means you are distanced from what's going on. And if you're not fully present, there's little you can do to change what is happening to you.

Moreover, the person who is giving you a hard time can keep heaping it on because they're not getting any response. They may even at some point realise that they're not making any impact and so step up the pressure; but you'll just wait till the storm is over before returning to the real world.

Absenting yourself from the fray is, of course, a version of flight. But we've given it a separate heading, as it is so common and used by so many people who aren't even aware they're doing it. At least if you walk out of a room or back down from an argument you know you're doing it. When you go into a dream world or switch off altogether, it is usually so automatic that you don't know what you've done or that it has created more problems for you.

Since this type of behaviour can be difficult to identify for yourself, you may need to ask someone who knows you well and whom you trust whether this is something you do when under pressure or attack. If you've been operating with a flight strategy for most of your life, then staying present will be a daunting thing to do in the face of someone's anger, demands, criticism, desires, thoughtlessness, etc.

I wish I didn't feel this way: being in charge vs being in control

Having looked at some of the ways you feel when you are being too nice, it is important for you to accept that there isn't a right way for you to feel. How can there be? And yet, that is what we imagine: that there are feelings we're *supposed* to have as opposed to the feelings that we *do* have. We hear people say things such as: 'I wish I didn't get upset when I get told off' or 'If only I didn't feel like crying when someone bullies me' or 'I wish my stomach didn't get butterflies when I have to stand up for myself'.

We also hear people say, 'I ought to be able to handle myself better.' 'I should be able to defend myself.' 'I should feel better about saying what I feel.' 'I ought not to feel like this at my age.'

Phrases like these are a self-imposed tyranny. You are telling yourself that you 'ought' to be different from how you actually are. These phrases are, in an ironic sense, a way to fool yourself: if you just tried hard enough you could change the way you feel about a situation. That's absurd.

There are many many things we have control over in our lives. Feelings aren't one of them. We can change how we react to our feelings, we can change what we do in response to our feelings and we can change what we think about our feelings. But the one thing we can't do, is change the feeling.

This is what we mean by being in charge vs being in control.

When things go wrong it may seem as though we're always getting the wrong end of the stick; and everyone else is getting the good end of it. Being in charge of your feelings simply means that ultimately you can handle whatever end of the stick you get.

At times we all wish we could control the way situations happen. We can't. You can't know what's going to happen. You can't know what your physical reactions are going to be until they happen. The bottom line is that things happen over which we have no control. In the real world you need to have the resources to deal with the stick ends as opposed to wishing you didn't have to deal with the stick at all.

Think of a time when you were just outright scared. It could have been someone creeping up on you and shouting 'Boo!' or it could have been something quite serious and really frightening such as a car crash, witnessing a horrible accident, being a victim of a crime or seeing your child in danger. Whatever the situation, your flight or fight mechanism would have reacted very strongly and produced feelings you could not possibly have had any control over.

Now remember what you actually did at the time. Did you shriek, cry, faint, tremble, go into shock, laugh a lot, babble, get angry?

Which do you think you have more control over? Not the feelings. They just happen without any say-so on your part. What you can start to change is how well you're in charge of what happens next. How you choose to think, react and behave when you have those feelings.

Feelings are your friend

Trying to be in control of your feelings is like trying to say that you don't have any at all. Feelings are a good thing to have. They are an indicator that you are alive! You may hate the feelings you have when you find yourself, once again, being too nice and getting taken advantage of, but they are telling you loud and clear that you don't like what's happening to you.

If you try to change your behaviour without acknowledging that these powerful feelings exist and affect you, you won't be able to do it. It's like a moth fluttering against a windowpane it can't see. You might learn all manner of techniques and skills to use in the face of bullying or emotional blackmail, but if you use them on top of unacknowledged feelings, they are unlikely to work well for you and soon you will slip right back into your old behaviour patterns.

Since it's your reactions that are really running the show not your feelings, techniques are worthless if you haven't done sufficient work on sorting out the difference between a feeling and a reaction!

Start with the feelings as a place to gather information about what is going on for you. They are a clear signal that something isn't right. If your reactions stay the same as they've always been, then they'll just perpetuate the same sense of victimisation and powerlessness. Your reactions come out of your historical responses to similar situations, your expectation of what always happens to you and your fears that nothing will ever change.

Most people believe that their reactions are more real than the feelings themselves. Your reactions do not tell you what is happening; your feelings do. Start with the feeling, not the reaction. Then you can play with how you decide you're going to react this time.

You can begin to look at this straight away, the next time you are put in an emotionally compromising situation. When you find yourself being too nice yet again and are beginning to react, see if you can stay conscious long enough to notice your body reactions. One of the first places to look is at your breathing. It is impossible to have a strong physical reaction to something without your breathing being affected.

Next, notice your heartbeat. Undoubtedly it will be accelerated as your body reacts to the stress. Then notice any other physical manifestations, such as sweating palms or trembling legs.

The more often you observe and note your physical state, the more clearly you will be able to identify the feelings that accompany it. Are you angry, hurt, frustrated, fearful? Take time to identify the exact feelings – put a name to them.

The longer your attention is on what you are feeling, the more time you will have before you react to those feelings. In this way you give yourself more time to choose how you are going to react. This will make more sense when you get to Part 2 where we look at some of the practical things that you can do to create more choice in your life. Right now, you will feel that the way you currently react is the only way available to you.

Since your body is doing its very best to prepare you for fight or flight, what if you looked upon all these feelings as good things to have instead of thinking of them as betrayers of your self-control? What if all these powerful feelings were telling you that you were in the right time and place to try something new?

With practice you can even begin to be on the lookout for feelings, rather than trying to hide from them. This means that when the feelings arise you know you now have a choice to make – the feelings are alerting you to the opportunity to choose differently. You can begin to look on feelings as allies; they can help you be more in charge of difficult situations instead of being a burden and an embarrassment.

4

NOT NICE/NOT NASTY: ENTERING THE MIDDLE GROUND

Nasty

We've spent the last three chapters looking at the nice you: exactly how nice you are, how you got that way and how your feelings of fear and anxiety keep you from changing.

But what about the other side of the spectrum? What about the 'nasty' you? This side of your personality doesn't get much of a look-in most of the time. This is the part of yourself you may be ashamed of because when it does get let out it seems out of your control.

Nasty is what happens to you when you are nice and compliant for far longer than you really want to be until you are no longer able to hold your resentment in. You lose control nastily and inappropriately all over whoever happens to be around.

This is the part of you that every once in a while simply goes on an emotional rampage, often for the most trivial of reasons. It is fed every time you give in to what other people want, and you resent this. You get bullied at work or by your partners or parents, and you resent it. You say yes when you mean no, and you resent it. You make things all right for everyone but yourself, and when your storehouse of resentment and anger has been fed beyond its capacity, the nasty you puts in an unplanned appearance.

Sometimes the rage only happens inside your head and remains unexpressed, while you seethe and boil internally. Other times the mild-mannered you becomes, however briefly, a raving lunatic as you express your anger in the most inappropriate places and in the most inappropriate ways. You go completely out of control. You 'lose it', 'go into a blind rage', 'see red'; 'fly off the handle'; 'blow your top' or whatever apt description you can find to describe what happens to you.

Anger is one of the most natural and useful emotions we have. As discussed in Chapter 2, infants express their anger – usually through crying – in order to get their needs and wants seen to. Anger as a tool of communication is preverbal. Like fear, it is a basic, instinctive feeling that alerts you when a boundary has been crossed or tells you that something isn't right.

Anger is a way of letting other people know that you're not happy with something they've said or something they've done. If we are offended, indignant, provoked, infuriated, hurt or frustrated, anger is a natural and necessary response to these emotions.

The expression of anger does not mean hitting someone, it does not mean smashing plates against the wall, it does not mean having a screaming fit at someone: only suppressed anger is usually expressed that way. Anger, expressed when it occurs, and in a relevant way, can simply be letting the other person know how hurt, upset, frustrated etc you really are.

Yes, there are times when a good old shout is a great release; and sometimes, as well, we get angry at intangible things like politics or the weather and we need to let off steam about those. We get angry at global crises that we seem to have no control over, such as endless battles in Bosnia and Iraq, the massacres in Rwanda, cancer, AIDS or the destruction of the rainforest.

But the anger we are talking about as it relates to nice people is the anger that rarely gets expressed at the right time and in the right place. This is the anger you might feel when someone takes you for granted, teases you unmercifully, takes advantage of your good nature, makes demands as a matter of course or disregards your feelings. This is the anger you might feel, but will rarely express to the person at the time it is happening.

If you've been practising the suppression of anger since you were little, you'll be especially adept at hiding it as an adult. You swallow the hurts, turn away from the insults; you may even deny that you feel angry at all. Many people never show their anger, but nobody *never* gets angry.

Restrained anger festers. The longer it festers, the bigger it grows;

and of course the bigger it grows, the more space it needs. Until finally, one day, there's no more room and all that suppression and sublimation gets knocked out of the way and the anger comes whooshing out. 'Where did that come from?' you might say to yourself as this rage takes control and knocks you out of the way as well.

Except that it's no longer as simple as saying, for instance, 'You know, I was really angry that you didn't include me in that strategy meeting yesterday; I feel it was really important for me to have been there.' Instead, a swamp of resentment will froth out at some distant time in the future, probably not even directed at the person who was the original cause of it. You get swept up in a tidal wave of emotion that causes you to behave in ways you will later regret.

I don't know what happened, something just came over me

John's story is a good example of what we mean.

> John is a very caring guy. Too caring. He'll do anything for anyone and appears to do it cheerfully. If Daniel, his lover, needs a shirt ironed at the last minute because he forgot to do one the night before, John will be late for his own job (he's a computer technician) to do it for him; if his parents ring him up at the last minute and ask him to take them shopping, John will put his own plans aside and drive over; if his brother mentions that he has no one to go with to watch his young nephew's football match on Saturday, John will go along even though he hates football; at work if there's a crash on someone's computer, his fellow technicians all turn to John because he's so good in a crisis and off he goes to sort out the problem.
>
> Everyone knows what a good egg John is; he'll do anything for you, and he usually ends up doing just that. Because John never mentions to anyone that he doesn't want to iron the shirt, do the shopping, watch football or fix the blasted computer, he keeps getting asked. And the more he's asked, the more he resents it. He can't believe

that people don't see how overworked he is and how he'd like someone to consider him for a change. But people deal with what he shows them which is that he likes to do things for people.

It wouldn't be so bad if he could say no every once in a while, but he can't even do that, so the resentment just builds and builds without an outlet.

Every now and then however, something happens which John can't figure out for the life of him. He explodes. He thinks he's fine, everything is going along smoothly and then he snaps. And always in the most unexpected circumstances.

Once he was in a shop buying some office supplies, the shop assistant wasn't being very helpful and John became enraged, spewing forth a terrible torrent of verbal abuse about her incompetence, how did she ever get a job in the first place, she has the IQ of a cucumber, and other words too impolite for this book. The tirade lasted for about five minutes, he stomped out of the shop and then it was over as quickly as it began, like a fierce tropical storm.

Walking down the street John felt awful, his head was filled with shameful thoughts: 'Should I go back and apologise?' 'Should I just go home and hide? I'll never be able to show my face in there again.' And of course, 'I don't know what happened, something just came over me.'

Another time when he was feeling particularly harassed, he interrupted a job he was concentrating on to pick up a persistently ringing phone in his department. It was someone from another department with an urgent computer crisis who needed someone to get up there right away. Without even thinking, John screamed, 'Fix your own bloody computer!' and slammed down the phone. Then he had to go back and proffer an abject, grovelling apology so that he wouldn't get the sack.

And finally, John was preparing for a dinner party with Daniel when he realised that Daniel had bought the wrong wine. That did it – John was in a rage about the wine, he couldn't trust Daniel to do anything right, the one little thing he'd asked him to do and he'd managed to screw it up.

But it didn't stop there. From out of nowhere Daniel heard about every wrongdoing for the past six months, including the unironed shirts. He heard about all the times he was late home from work without phoning, his bad driving, the fact that he ducked out of the Saturday football matches and that he was never interested in John's day.

Daniel reeled back from the onslaught but he also got reeled into an argument which had no place to go but escalation, indignation and finally tears. And as usual, John ended up apologising for what had come over him.

John represents the kind of person who is religiously nice and always accommodating, right up until they can't take it any more and then out of nowhere all the stored resentment gets expressed in totally inappropriate ways. Either an innocent bystander is the recipient or the guilty party is the recipient but over something completely unrelated to the incident that caused the anger in the first place.

Nice people can stay nice for only so long before something has to give. If they keep all that anger bottled up the bottle will explode and someone (usually the Johns of this world) will get hurt.

I never get angry

Sometimes the bottle can implode. By that we mean that the resentment and rage gets expressed inwardly instead of outwardly. The fury happens inside you, not in the real world. This is when you seethe about what is happening to you, but the storehouse of rage-filled feelings stays locked within you. You might plot revenge, torture or murder but no hint of that ever passes your lips.

You suffer in total silence. Not even if you are severely provoked will you let anyone know of the raging turmoil that's going on inside of you. All the dialogue is happening internally. If you comment at all you might use phrases such as 'I was a bit annoyed'; 'It was no big deal'; 'I'm sure he didn't mean it'; 'It was a bit inconvenient'. Or you might say, 'Yes, I was a bit annoyed when…'; 'It was somewhat irritating…'; 'I was a bit cross…' It's always a bit cross, annoyed, etc, rather than 'I was really angry when…'

Annoying is when you can't find a parking space or your dry cleaning isn't ready on time or your meeting goes on longer than expected and you're late for the theatre. Irritating is when you've been waiting for a bus in the rain for 25 minutes or your child upends your neatly folded laundry and scatters it all over the sitting room. Irritation and annoyance are very real emotions but they are not anger.

You might be the type of person who is so distanced from your feelings that you don't realise how very upset you really are. On our workshops we have heard people tell the most horrendous stories of what's happening in their daily lives while smiling and voicing enough justification of other people's behaviour to qualify them as barristers.

Whichever you are, an exploder or an imploder, if you are not expressing your anger at the relevant times and places, then you are functioning under tremendous stress. We're not even saying that your anger needs to be verbalised at all times when a situation occurs to trigger it off. Sometimes self-restraint is a mature and appropriate response. But if it is never, or rarely, voiced then you are carrying quite a heavy load of feelings that have nowhere to go.

Another nice/nasty exercise

This is a short exercise for you to look at the two extremes of your behaviour: the nice you and the nasty you. You can do this exercise in your head; you can make lists; you can draw or doodle; you can do it with a friend: whatever medium you would like to play with is fine for this exercise. We do encourage drawing (which is about expression, rather than art, for all you people who are saying, 'I can't draw'), as it can tap into ideas and creativity which remain hidden a lot of the time.

If you can, get yourself comfortable; stretch a bit to get some of the kinks out and even give a yawn or two. Then take two or three deep breaths in, breathing in and then holding the breath for a few seconds and letting it out in a big whoosh.

Now imagine a blank cinema screen or a blank sheet of paper or an empty stage. Onto that stage or screen or on that paper picture yourself as a **nice** person. This is you when you are accommodating, pleasing, turning away from slights, making it all right for other people, giving in, giving up.

The image could be an actual scene from your life – a recent or even an old event where being too nice left you feeling disempowered and victimised. The image could be colours or shapes or a symbol. You might imagine phrases that people say to you or words that come out of your mouth when you're being too nice. Whatever comes up for you is fine.

Next, let that image fade and bring to the screen, paper or stage, an image of you as a **nasty** person. This is you when you've had it. When you can't take it any more and you explode, either internally or externally. This is when all those resentments and unvoiced angry feelings are given full vent and you let rip. Again, this might be a recent or past time when you've expressed all those feelings verbally and gone out of control or kept it all inside but had raging, furious thoughts.

The image might simply be shapes or colours; and as with the nice image, you might imagine phrases that come up for you or that get said to you when you're in this state. Whatever image appears is good for this exercise.

Now bring the two images together side by side: the nice you on one side and the nasty on the other. If you are able to take the time, draw, make a list, doodle or describe what images came up for you. What did you see or hear? How do you see yourself as each of those extremes of behaviour?

Is this all there is?

For many nice people, the extremes of behaviour are the only ones they experience in themselves: nice, compliant, accommodating and pleasing; or nasty, raging, over-the-top and out-of-control. Most nice people feel that that is how the world really is: you can either be nice (most of the time) or you can be nasty (occasionally).

Neither state can possibly be consistently effective. But, as you know, whatever degree of nice you are, that isn't all there is, no matter how much it may seem like that at times. Otherwise you wouldn't have those conversations in your head about what you might have said if only you had had the courage.

The fact that you often actually know what you'd like to do or say is a clear indication that you're well aware that there are different options than the ones you end up taking. That your feelings stop you from acting the way you'd like doesn't minimise the knowledge you have that being nice or nasty isn't all there is.

We have an extremely simple model which illustrates our view of the whole spectrum of possible behaviour.

Picture #1: This is a diagram showing how most nice people see themselves in the world, as we have just described. There is nice and there is nasty.

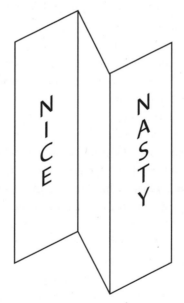

Picture #2: This is a diagram which opens up to show that there is indeed nice and nasty at the two ends of the picture, but in the middle there is a huge area which we have called 'not nice' but also 'not nasty' or in other words, the Middle Ground.

```
┌─────────────────────────────────────────┐
│         100% of possible behaviour       │
├──────┬──────────────────────────┬────────┤
│      │        NOT NICE          │        │
│  N   │                          │  N     │
│  I   │                          │  A     │
│  C   │                          │  S     │
│  E   │                          │  T     │
│      │        NOT NASTY         │  Y     │
├──────┴──────────────────────────┴────────┤
│           MIDDLE GROUND                   │
│        ◄──────────────────►               │
```

We have deliberately included both the nice and nasty ends because we see the entire range as 100 per cent of the way you could behave in order to have a more effective life.

We'll explain this model in more detail. If we just stay with the two ends for the moment, what we'll look at is what you already know about expressing nice or nasty behaviour.

If you are nice, *when you don't choose to be,* you know what you're going to get: you're going to be put upon, you're going to go out of your way to please people, you're going to be taken advantage of, you're going to defer to others. This means you're going to feel angry, frustrated, hurt, minimised, pained, etc. You might feel invisible or very small. You'll feel powerless and incapable of breaking out of that powerlessness. It may even feel at times as though the world is conspiring against you.

You'll do the school-run five days in a row; you'll take on extra work because no one else will; you'll feel obliged to talk to the party bore so he won't feel left out; you'll say it's OK when someone changes plans on you at the last minute for the fourth or fifth time.

Having stayed in the nice end of the spectrum for a long time, you will have started to build up your storehouse of resentment, frustration and anger which will then get larger and larger. At some point you will have built up such a charge of intense feelings that, like lightning in a thunder storm, you will flip over into nasty behaviour as you discharge all that built-up nastiness in one fell swoop.

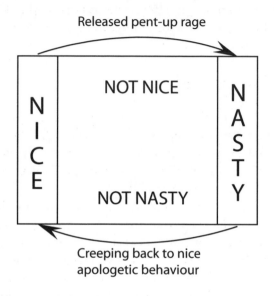

Released pent-up rage

Creeping back to nice
apologetic behaviour

If you are nasty, *when you don't choose to be*, you also know what you're going to get. You're going to create a big mess. People will be aghast at your behaviour, possibly saying, 'What's come over you?' You will have yelled and screamed, caused a huge scene and frightened people with your unexpected aggression.

You will then, when the storm has died down, have to apologise, prostrate yourself, placate the offended party, make amends and will end up scurrying back to nice behaviour as fast as you possibly can.

Unlike the nice end where you are invisible, at this end you will be super-visible, larger than life. For a while, it feels an incredibly powerful place to be. The only problem is that because you didn't consciously choose to use nasty behaviour, you're probably not very conscious about what is happening.

We know that when you are being too nice you will often be operating with your antennae at full extension, on super-alert for potential problems. It's as though your eyes are very wide open observing life around you at a 360 degree angle, taking in everything.

When you are nasty, you very often have your eyes shut tight, so you're not really seeing what's going on.

When you're nice, you're over-responsible. When you're nasty, you say you're not responsible for your actions because you don't know what came over you. When you're nice, you give and care too much; when you're nasty, you're beyond caring.

The middle ground

Living in one end or the other is limiting, and it certainly narrows the possibilities you have to be more in charge of your life. While you stay in the nice end and occasionally surge over to the nasty end, you are ignoring the vast range of behaviour in the middle, which we have earlier called 'not nice' and 'not nasty'.

While you know what you'll get by remaining in the two ends, when you are in the middle ground you haven't any real idea of what might happen. You may step out of your normal way of behaving and discover that no one notices. You may step out of the nice end and find that people want to shove you right back in. And you may edge your way into the middle ground and encounter a nasty person when you least expect it. You could get exactly what you want, you could get half of what you want, you could get none of what you want. You simply do not know.

In the middle ground you are vulnerable because you have stepped square into the unknown. All those defence mechanisms are gearing themselves up to protect you. In general, most people don't like to feel vulnerable. It can feel very exposed to step out of your normal way of behaving into a place where you say what you want.

Since you have spent a good part of your life from early childhood trying to create certainty by predicting, by hedging your bets, by trying to control what could happen to you, moving into this new territory could be a most frightening experience: stepping out into a new place where you do not know what's going to happen will surely evoke feelings of being out of control and not knowing what's the right thing to do.

What we do know is that it often appears easier for people to stay in the nice end of the spectrum, building up a volatile charge of frustration, hurt and despair, flip over into the nasty side to discharge it all and then sprint back again, than it is to step even a tiny way into the middle ground.

The fear of consequences is so overwhelming and the certainty you have about what's going to happen if you do is functioning in such high gear that you won't even be able to make that small move. This again is what we mean when we say you make it up and act as though it's true: you have already decided what will happen if you step into the middle ground, so you don't.

The middle ground is the place where you express your needs and wants; it's the place where you tell someone the effect they're having on you; it's where you disagree, speak your mind, say no, challenge, voice your anger or disappointment, refuse to turn the other cheek. As you will read in the chapters ahead, the middle ground is where the true art of saying no happens.

Being 'not nice' and 'not nasty' means telling your boss you can't possibly stay late tonight, saying to your mother you don't want her to ring you every day, telling your flatmate it's her turn to do the washing-up for the next week, turning an overstaying house-guest out on the street, letting the party bore know you're not interested, refusing to take sides in a family argument that's been going on for 10 or 20 years.

In the middle ground it's more difficult to be ruled by the imperatives of obligation, duty, guilt, have tos, oughts and shoulds. It's more difficult to be ruled by rules, because all the ones you've created to help get you through don't apply any more.

We also want to remind you of what we were saying in Chapter 3 about all those uncomfortable feelings being a good place to be since they are indicating to you that something new is happening and you have a chance to make a different choice. That is what going into the middle ground is really all about: having a whole range of heightened feelings and making a different choice.

As we have mentioned in Chapter 1 in discussing degrees of niceness, there may be times in your life when you are not nice; whole areas where you don't have any problem stepping into the middle ground at all. Since this book is for anyone who recognises overly nice behaviour as a problem, we leave it to you to identify when you have the most difficulty moving into the unknown.

You might even want to give some thought to what the difference is when you can and when you can't move into the middle ground: what's easy, what's difficult, what's impossible.

For some people, complaining in a restaurant never presents a problem – if the soup is cold, send it back. For others, just the idea of voicing even the mildest complaint will fill them with panic. Those same restaurant complainers may well freeze when it comes to asking their secretaries to do a pile of photocopying for them, because the secretary might get upset, while the person who panics in a restaurant won't think twice about giving orders at work – their secretary's upset doesn't bother them one whit.

This is what we mean when we say everyone is nice in a different way and will react to different situations in completely unpredictable ways. Your way is yours. Your ability to enter or retreat from the middle ground will be particular to you.

Since most nice people tend to operate in extremes and are continually looking for the right rules of behaviour, we can hear some of you assuming that the *only* place to be is the middle ground; that the correct way to behave is to step into the unknown no matter what.

Staying in either end of the behavioural spectrum exclusively diminishes who you are. However, to now think that you have to be brave and courageous and stand your middle ground all the time is equally diminishing.

There are times when it is important and very useful to be nice. We like our nice selves: the caring, generous, thoughtful people who do look out for others' well being. We wouldn't be doing this kind of work if we weren't nice. We certainly wouldn't want to eradicate that part of our personalities for the sake of having more confidence or self-assurance.

In turn, being nasty also has an important function. If we're being abused or trodden on, we need to be able to roll upon our very nasty sides in order to stop it from happening.

Again, this is why we see our model as representing 100 per cent of behaviour. We want to be able to operate comfortably with all the possibilities, so that our new diagram looks like this.

NICE

NOT NICE

NASTY

NOT NASTY

The rev counter

Here's another diagrammatic way of looking at this. Those of you who drive will know that in some cars there is a rev counter (not the speedometer which calculates speed, the rev counter calculates the revolutions the engine is making when it's on). A rev counter will be a version of the diagram below.

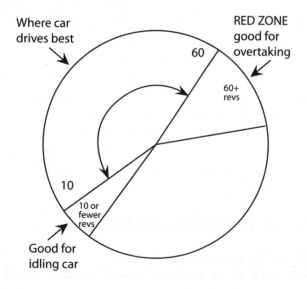

Where car drives best

RED ZONE good for overtaking

60

60+ revs

10

10 or fewer revs

Good for idling car

Some rev counters delineate the rev speed in three sections: a small section at the lower end (0–20 revs); a large section in the middle (20–60 revs) and generally a Red Zone (60+ revs). When your car is warming up or idling at traffic lights or sitting in a traffic jam, the engine will be in first gear and will be turning over at low revs. When you need to overtake another car you might put the car in third gear and then step on the accelerator for a very short time – and the revs will speed up during the manoeuvre.

Try putting your car in third or fourth gear from a standing start and stepping on the accelerator: nothing will happen other than stalling the car. If you shift into first or second gear and step on the accelerator to red zone rev speed, you'll blow up the engine if you stay there too long.

You need to be able to idle in traffic and drive slowly and carefully at times, just as you need to be able to speed up and get yourself moving forward really fast. But not all the time. To drive the car most effectively and efficiently, you need to be driving so that the engine is revving in the middle.

Being nice and nasty is a bit like that. You might put a lot of effort in, but if the car is stuck in low revs (eg you're still being accommodating, giving in, putting up with) you're not going to go anywhere, no matter how much energy you throw at the problem. You might 'flip over' into nasty and express all your rage and get it out of your system, but in the meantime you've blown up the engine with the scorched-earth theory of problem solving and you have to go get it fixed, which in your case means being back into low-rev nice.

All rev speeds are necessary, just as the full spectrum of behaviour is necessary. When you drive most of you will automatically know which gear to choose when, how much pressure to put on the accelerator, when to brake, when to overtake, when to slow down. That is what we hope you will be able to take away from this book – how to function through all the choices you have: when to stay nice, when to get nasty and when to enter the middle ground.

Becoming more burglar-proof

Here's yet another way to look at this issue.

Let's say you're a burglar. There's a row of identical terraced houses you're thinking of having a go at, five of them. The first house has a Yale lock on the front door. The second house has a Yale and a Chubb lock on the front door. The third house has a Yale and a Chubb lock on the front door and bars on the windows. The fourth house has the Yale and Chubb locks, bars on the windows and a burglar alarm. And the fifth has the Yale and Chubb locks, bars on the windows, a burglar alarm **and** a Rottweiler.

Which would you burgle?

That's what we're looking at here. What we know about nice people is that they will attract emotional burglars. Because they are unprotected, because they don't know how to move into the middle ground effectively, because, in essence, they seem like sitting ducks to a lot of other people, they will be burgled more frequently.

You need to become more burglar-proof, by which we mean that the more you practise alternative behaviour, the less attractive you will become to burglars. You don't have to go all the way by having the burglar alarm and the Rottweiler. Most of the time the extra lock and the occasional bar on the window is all the protection you need (ie moving only a short way into the middle ground); occasionally, however, you need to haul in the Rottweiler either for show or to give the offender a really good scare (ie moving to the nasty end of the spectrum).

What we have discovered personally and in the stories we hear at Impact Factory, is that if someone is used to taking advantage of you and you put up no resistance, they'll keep doing it; if you put up some resistance, they'll go find somebody else to do it to.

People who know how to get their own needs and wants taken care of are very good at it – that's what *they've* been practising all their lives. They operate through the gears of their lives automatically. They aren't necessarily thinking, 'Now how can I take advantage of this nice person.' What they do is look around and decide who's going to be the most accommodating to their wishes.

Choose me

You are subliminally giving out signals to people that say it's all right to take advantage. In the last chapter we talked about the physical responses you have when you are in a stressful situation. These physical indicators are telling other people that you're a pushover.

They may not consciously know it, but when they need someone to bake extra cakes for the local fête they'll think of you rather than the woman down the lane; when, at five minutes to six, they need someone to pick up the 'governor' from across town, they'll choose you instead of one of your colleagues who's sitting right next to you; when they need someone to take minutes at the PTA meeting, they'll say 'You don't mind, do you?' without thinking twice about it.

So the overstaying house-guest isn't necessarily deliberately taking advantage of you, they've just looked down their list of friends and decided you'd be good to stay with because they always have a good time when they stay with you. And if every once in a while they have to stay on longer than expected, well, you've always been great and never given them a hard time about it, so it must not bother you.

Similarly, the kind of party bore who has a really thick skin and likes the sound of his own voice (who most likely doesn't know he's that boring) isn't consciously deciding on whom to inflict his tedium; but he'll look around the room and search for a sympathetic face – yours – who he knows on a subconscious level will listen to him.

You, yourself, make similar choices all the time. You'll be attracted to certain people (both on positive and negative levels) because of the signals they transmit. The difference for you is that when someone comes along and chooses you, you may not be able to say, 'No thank you, please choose someone else' as you get stuck yet again doing something you don't want to be doing.

A number of years ago there was a study carried out in New York City with an ex-mugger and a Laban notator (Labanotation is a two-dimensional way of recording the movements of people). This ex-mugger pointed out the people he would have chosen to mug and the notator recorded the movements of the people he designated. This went on for quite some time till they had a sizeable collection of records.

The mugger hadn't thought about his choices – he just chose. And what was discovered at the end of the exercise is that every person he chose moved in a similar fashion: they were top-heavy and looked as though they could be pushed over easily. The study wasn't undertaken to prove that only these types of people got mugged, but it gave important information in helping people become less muggable: stride, walk as though you are well grounded, move with assurance.

Nothing surprising in that information; it's very logical, even without the study to back it up. Just as it's very logical to say to nice people, 'Just say no' as though that will fix the problem. That advice, however, is a lot harder to put into practice than adopting a strong walk.

The only way you are going to become more burglar-proof is to practise enough alternative forms of behaviour to the ones you use which continue to create all the helpless, unhappy and stuck feelings that you currently experience.

You do not, however, have to change it all. As a matter of fact, you have to change very little. We wrote in the Introduction 'the least amount of change for the greatest impact' because if you are faced with the daunting and impossible task of having to change your whole personality you won't do it. You may have an image of yourself transformed into this incredibly assured, outspoken person able to handle yourself in all situations no matter what.

It's not going to happen. You aren't going to get transformed. What we hope you will be able to do is to make enough small changes, produce enough minor adjustments and alter enough of your reactions to difficult situations so that your life will be a happier place to be.

One man said to us a number of months after doing The Nice Factor course that he had expected such huge changes that people would be gasping at how different he had become and be impressed at the way he had suddenly taken charge of his life. Instead, what he found is that no one really noticed the changes because they were subtle and for the most part, internal – he was the only one who really knew what was going on. But, interestingly enough, his life was better; things were easier; there was less struggle.

As you read Part 2 which is all about 'what next?' see if you can keep that in mind. Small changes, easy and fun to put into practice, will make the difference, rather than trying to become someone you aren't.

Summary

For us, becoming conscious of your behaviour, your feelings and your fears is the first major step in liberating yourself from the tyranny of being too nice for your own good.

Before you have even started on the techniques and tools we've collected in Part 2, you will have already begun the process of change. You will have heightened your awareness of what you do and how you feel; once you bring something into awareness, you can't suddenly become unaware of it.

Are there things you now notice that you hadn't necessarily noticed before: not just what you do, but *other* people's behaviour as well? Do you notice how many times you or someone else says 'I'm sorry' when there's nothing to be sorry about; or have you noticed other people telling you how you feel and what you want or don't want without consulting you on your view of the situation; or perhaps you've now become aware that there are certain people who want you to stay nice because it makes their life easier.

The more you develop your awareness, the better you will become at choosing the behaviour you want to display when you want to display it.

We believe that it takes courage to be willing to do the kind of soul-searching you have just completed, so congratulations are due to yourself from yourself, as well as from us.

Part 2

The Art of Saying No: Getting Your Choice Back

Introduction

We talked in Chapter 2 about how originally becoming nice was a choice, even if it didn't feel much like one at the time. If you chose it once, you do have the ability to 'unchoose' it now, or at least to start making different choices.

The rest of this book covers what some of those choices might be and how you could put them into effect. We don't intend them to be a 'how to' in the classic sense, such as 'follow these ten steps and you will suddenly become less nice'. It doesn't work that way.

The art of saying no isn't something you can learn out of a textbook. An art is something you practise; you make mistakes, practise again, refine. An art evolves and, in time, becomes more like second-nature.

We will be presenting the techniques, methods and skills that we work with in our workshops, but for us they are ways of highlighting new possibilities rather than giving you the right way to be 'not nice'.

We say again, there is no *right* way; there are *different* ways. There are even ways in which you currently behave that could be adjusted just enough to make them work for you. Just finding one or two changes that really suit you will make a tremendous difference.

We also want to introduce a cornerstone of our work here, which is about **playing life more like a game.**

Being too nice is no joke. When you are in the midst of dread, shame or rage, it can feel deadly serious. We do not want to make light of the consequences that you fear or the difficulties that you experience. We've heard quite sad and disturbing histories of people who have a huge degree of disharmony and dis-ease in their lives because they've been so accommodating and so unable to put themselves first, even occasionally.

However, because it is so serious and there are indeed serious consequences to this type of behaviour, all of us sometimes lose sight of the fact that there is a whole lot of delightful life going on around us. Therefore, we will be bringing lightness and humour, when appropriate, into the process of change throughout the rest of the book.

By this we don't mean for you to pretend to things you aren't feeling or to laugh off insults or other people's bad behaviour; you've been doing that for long enough as it is. But through practising some of the options we present, we hope a sense of play, humour and lightness will be instilled. We hope that you will find things that are fun to do.

We know that changing behaviour is one of the most difficult things to do. Because this problem has been ingrained since early childhood, changing patterns of compliance on whatever level will be met with resistance both by yourself and by many people in your life. Family and friends like you nice: it makes life easy for them.

As well as possibly being confronted with resistance from all sides, you may find yourself confronted with your own resistance: your own uncomfortable and painful feelings. The body is the repository of many unpleasant memories. You may logically know what to do and understand why that's the best way forward; but it is your body that will react to change with knots in your stomach, tightness in your throat, accelerated heartbeat, etc.

Sometimes the messes we get into are hard to believe when looked at objectively. 'How on earth did I manage to get myself into this fix?' we say. When you can see the humorous side of a situation you've got yourself into, you're in a better position to wrest back some of the power and control you have so unwittingly given to other people. Then you have more of a chance to do something to change the situation.

What we've done is to create a series of exercises, processes and ideas that are game-like. Over the next few chapters you'll be looking at how to put these game-like situations into practice, except that you'll be the only player in the game. That's the interesting thing: no one will know you're doing it other than you. Other people might have a sense of the results being different from the way things normally work out with you, but when you're the only player in the game, you actually have quite a lot of power and it can be a lot of fun.

One of the main purposes of looking at these scenarios in a game-like fashion is so that when you put them into practice in the real world, the real world won't have such a serious edge to it.

We also know that the more fun we can make the process of change, the easier it is to enter into that process. We hope you will try to tackle this seemingly impossible task from an enjoyable perspective. We want you to relish the challenges of change rather than feeling it's going to be like climbing Mt Everest without a Sherpa guide. Start with small hills, leave Everest to the more experienced!

Another cornerstone to our work is about **getting small wins**.

We use this term a lot: small wins. If you go into a situation trying to change everything you do and face your worst demons it is likely that you will fail. We're not saying don't try it, but if you could pull it off, you most likely would have already. At the beginning of taking on something new, beginner steps are a good idea.

As you accumulate enough little victories that are relatively easy to accomplish, then when you begin to feel able to tackle the really big issues, you will have collected enough experiences to give you the self-confident edge you need. Practising on the issues that cause you the most pain and that you dread the most isn't going to be fun, it isn't going to be easy and the most likely result is that you'll be put off doing it.

We will be presenting you with some fun challenges that won't throw you into the lion's den just yet but will get you started on your collection of wins.

On our workshops participants bring in scenarios that we revisit in order to see what other choices they could have made to affect a different outcome. These are situations that have happened in their lives where being too nice left them feeling disempowered, angry, frustrated and with a sense of having 'lost'.

Here, we are going to use scenarios that we have seen and worked with over the years. They are the best way to illustrate some of the methods, ideas and techniques that we use, playing with a variety of possible outcomes.

In each of these scenarios we have selected from a 'grab bag' of actions and tools to have the person practise with. However, there were any number of possibilities we could have chosen; what we looked at was what was possible for that person at that time. We don't say that this is the way the person 'ought' to have dealt with the problem; rather this was a way they *could* have dealt with it. This is what we mean when we talk about refining the art of saying no: There can be no one right way; you can only refine your way and find out what will work for you best.

In the same way, when you begin to think about yourself in similar situations (and we know that many of the scenarios will look very familiar to you), it is vital to remember that there is always more than one choice. There will be methods we suggest where you will say to yourself, 'I could never do that' in the same way there will be other suggestions where you will say, 'Yes! That one I'll try.'

A note about families

As you have already read in previous chapters, this book is filled with a variety of scenarios and situations that people encounter in their daily lives. Some of them present more difficult challenges than others.

One area where we know the most difficulty can occur is in dealing with families. Your family will present problems that are unique to you. However, it is important to keep a couple of things in mind when you read through the scenarios and solutions that we present in the next few chapters.

1. Every family is different. On a logical level you already know that; but when it comes to changing your behaviour in relation to your family, no one technique or example that we include here is going to automatically work for you. You probably tolerate behaviour from family members that you wouldn't consider (even in your nicest state) tolerating from friends or colleagues.

2. Patterns of communication. What happens in families is that, patterns of communication are established (in most cases long before you were born) and stay that way – seemingly for ever. You will have adapted to these patterns as naturally as learning to walk and talk. You had no other option.

Therefore, if you have any hope of changing these well-entrenched habits and expectations, something different *on your part* is going to have to happen.

3. 'I just want them to understand.' There will be some situations where radical action is needed to shift old, established patterns. There will be other situations, however, that may require a lighter touch and indeed may require all the love and understanding you can muster, even though what you want to do is demand that they understand you. We wouldn't count on it if we were you.

So many people want their parents to understand who and what they are and they figure if they just try hard enough to explain their parents will 'get it' one day. Unlikely.

Given that, you need to decide how far you're willing to go and for what results. If you're looking for understanding you may need to look elsewhere. If you're looking to change the way you and your family members communicate, then many of the tips we offer in this book will be very useful and doable. Tact and sensitivity may provide a far better outcome when combined with some of the techniques we describe.

5

I'm Sorry:
How Language Keeps You Stuck

Can language be too nice?

Oddly enough, one of the first places to start when looking to change your behaviour is language. That may seem a bit strange if ultimately what you want to do is to alter your adaptive and accommodating behaviour. However, it's not so strange as all that.

Think about it for a moment. Go back over the memories you've had when doing some of the earlier exercises in this book. Things that were said to you will have affected you as much if not more than what was actually done. Now, we aren't trying to minimise what *was* done, and some of you may have experienced a great deal of physical abuse, some of it horrific. But language creates the climate within which it is hard to do anything other than modify your natural self.

In the chapter on childhood we highlighted some of the ways in which parents control their children. Some of the most effective ways are to bully, harass or humiliate children by putting them down, minimising what they feel or want, insisting that they think and behave the way the parents want them to; it can all be done through language without a hint of physical violence to be seen.

Indeed, most of you will have had an experience in school, for instance, of being singled out and humiliated by your teacher in front of your peers. This might have been for being naughty, answering a question incorrectly, weeing in your pants, daydreaming, failing an exam, being late, etc. That kind of public humiliation is usually enough to ensure that you will do whatever it takes to avoid a repeat of that sense of shame and embarrassment.

Not only that, there will be some of you who only had to witness that being done to someone else to ensure you stayed in line. Just the thought of that kind of public verbal censure was enough to keep you in your place.

Words. Words shape the way you think and the way you see the world.

Language is one of the most potent shapers of behaviour that we have at our disposal. Words were used to get you to be how others wanted you to be: they were used to belittle, to threaten, to promise and reward, to intimidate and frighten, to persuade, to manipulate. Words can feel like a slap across the face; they wound our self-esteem, injure our pride.

Language seeps into our psyches because we hear things before we have the understanding of their true meaning. Things are said to us by people we revere or fear or are in awe of and we take them as truths long before we have the capacity to doubt.

Painful and hurtful things were said to you that are fixed in such a deep internal place that even now that you've learned to doubt and question, you doubt the doubt. It's hard to question whether your mother really meant it when, in exasperation, she told you, 'You're hopeless – what am I going to do with you?'

Language – things that were said to you – will have affected you enormously. That's why when we begin to look at ways to change your behaviour we begin with the word.

And the first place we begin is the simple things you say in apology. And what's the most common form of apology? 'I'm sorry.'

How much is your daily language sprinkled with 'I'm sorry'? What are you actually apologising for?

People apologise when they think they've done something wrong, of course; but they also apologise when someone bumps into them; they apologise when they feel they are acting out of turn; they apologise when they want to ask for something they think they won't get; they apologise for other people's behaviour; they apologise when someone else is upset; they apologise when there is absolutely no reason for apology.

Jo Ellen: I once had a friend stay in the cottage I used rent in the country. We were doing some housework together

and his foot brushed against a couple of bricks that were
holding up a piece of furniture.

'I'm sorry,' he said.

'You just apologised to a brick' I said.

'Oh,' he said, looking down, 'I'm sorry.'

Our use of language is a habit. In the same way that thinking we have
no choice becomes a habit, language is so automatic we don't even
know we're doing it most of the time.

**The use of language shapes and reinforces our beliefs and our sense
of self.**

In Chapter 4 we talked about becoming more burglar proof. One of
the things that will attract emotional burglars to you is the language
that you use. Body language can give a message to people that you are
'doormatable'. Spoken language has the same, if not more, power to do
so as well. You may be verbally cowering in the language you use.

Your language transmits powerful signals that give tacit permission
to other people that you are fair game. If you continually apologise or
use language that is vague, wishy-washy, unclear and indirect, you leave
yourself wide open for other people to misinterpret you, to ignore you
or to pretend you didn't really mean it anyway. You give them the tools
to bully you into doing things you don't want to do.

Along with apology is the perpetual asking for permission. Nice
people ask permission for everything, including whether it's all right to
ask permission. Asking permission means that you can be refused. Asking permission is a clear indicator to other people that you're not sure
whether it's all right, and it puts you in a subservient role.

The language of apology and permission is a kind of padding; a
buffer between what you want to say and what you actually do say. It's
as though your speech is encased in cotton wool so that the real intention is camouflaged.

The rest of this chapter is devoted to the specific words and phrases
that you use to transmit these signals to other people. We will be looking at them from a multilevel perspective, from the surface, day-to-day
habits of speech to the phrases and sayings that were lessons in
themselves and, even deeper, to some of the cultural language lessons
we get when we're very young.

Let's start with something simple.

Here is one of our favourite examples and it has to do with one of the 20th century's most successful gadgets: the answering machine. If you have one, what does yours say? If you don't, you have most likely rung others who have them – what do theirs say?

We felt very smug indeed when we were creating our original Nice Factor workshop because we each separately noticed that both our machines started off by apologising for us in our absence: 'I'm sorry, unfortunately, I'm not available to take your call…' 'I'm sorry'? 'Unfortunately'? We swiftly changed that part of our messages. Why should we apologise for not being available? What if we're not sorry we're not there to take your call? We might have been off doing wonderful things and the last thing we wanted was to be talking to anyone. Or maybe one of us was having a 'hide under the duvet' kind of day and couldn't be bothered.

But why apologise?

As we said, we were feeling quite smug and proud of ourselves for being so clever. It took us a few more months of leading our workshops before it dawned on each of us that we had only changed the beginning of our messages. The ends still said, 'Please leave a message and I'll get back to you as soon as possible.'

Wait a minute! Now our machines were making promises for us in our absence! What if we didn't want to get back to that person, ever, never mind as soon as possible? What if we were so busy that we wouldn't be able to get back to anybody for days? Why should we have machines that were making commitments for us? Not so smug this time, we changed the tail-ends of our messages.

Some answering machine manufacturers conspire in this as well. Some of them in their sample messages suggest apology and absent promises as the right kind of message to record. *And we go along with it without even thinking, it's so familiar and automatic.*

A big deal? Yes, we think it is. We've been told it's polite convention to have messages like that; it's common courtesy. Why? Why is it socially more acceptable to say 'I'm sorry I'm not available to take your call' than it is to say 'I'm not available to take your call'?

We put all this emphasis on answering machines because we think it's a clear indicator of how we accept blindly the right way to do things;

how we are subservient to what is expected of us. You are expected to be sorry that you're not there to take the call when someone wants you; you are expected to be prompt in getting back to people because they want you to be.

Language says something different about you. If you are someone who apologises constantly, your answering machine is a reflection of that and you can do something quite simple to change it. If you can begin to change the words that come out of your mouth automatically you will begin to change the way you feel about yourself and the way people react to you.

If your answering machine is one that tells the world you are sorry you aren't at their beck and call and then promises you'll put them first on the agenda when you finally do appear, changing your message is a good way to practise being 'not nice'. We think it's a brilliant first step.

The wonderful thing about changing your message is that it doesn't involve anyone else. You don't have to work up any courage to confront something or someone you've been avoiding. You don't have to challenge any fears or go to the edge of what's possible for you. You can also have some fun with this, thinking up an alternative. Jo Ellen's machine shocks some people now because it says, 'I'll get back to you when I get back to you.' Unheard of a few years ago.

This is your first small win. This is a win worth savouring because it will take you from the realm of the automatic into the realm of the conscious. If you don't have an apologetic message, then you can be smug and mention it to friends and family who do. Or if you're not brave enough to tell them straight out, make it game-like and keep a mental tally every time you hear someone else's machine being apologetic. Answering machines are just for starters.

The language of apology

Let's take an in-depth look at how the language of apology works and what words and phrases you use that condemn you without your even being aware of it.

First, there's day-to-day usage – the things that fall out of your mouth automatically. Second, will be the sayings and aphorisms you heard growing up that were the ground rules of your expected behaviour. Thirdly there are nursery rhymes and other childhood lessons that reinforced the teachings you got at home.

In each case, as in the first exercise in Chapter 1, mark on a scale of one to four how often you use or have heard the phrases we have listed: 1 – Never; 2 – Sometimes; 3 – Often; 4 – On a regular basis.

You can use the same measurement as in the first chapter to decide just how nice your language is, but this exercise is here to focus your attention on the way you habitually use language, how you say words and phrases automatically. Obviously, the more 3s and 4s you have, the more your language will be reflective of your nice behaviour and your beliefs about yourself.

Day-to-day usage

How do you apologise? What do you say when you ask someone to do something you think they won't want to do? What do you say when you have to give bad news? What words do you use when you want to introduce a new idea?

These are the little gems that affirm your invisibility and your second-class status. These are the words that tell other people you don't take yourself very seriously; that your wants, ideas, thoughts and feelings aren't that important. These are the ways you hedge your bets, just in case people already think that about you anyway (that you're stupid, pathetic, have nothing to say etc).

This is the language you use when you seek reassurance. They are also the self-deprecating remarks with which you put yourself down, bat away compliments.

I'm sorry.
I'm really terribly sorry.
Would you mind terribly?
Would it be possible if…
Yes.
But.
Yes, but…
Just.
Unfortunately.
Excuse me.

Is it all right if I...?
Do you mind if I...?
I'm not sure you're going to like this.
Would you do me a favour?
I don't want to impose...
Would you consider...?
This will probably sound pathetic.
I'm fine.
If it isn't too much trouble.
Do you think you might be able to...?
Sorry to interrupt, or, Do you mind if I interrupt?
You're not going to like this.
I couldn't do that.
Leave it to me, I'll take care of it.
I don't mind.
Fair enough.
Is that all right with you?
Don't ask me, I don't know anything.
I'm sorry to trouble you.
Please excuse the mess.
I have to apologise for...
I'm sorry to trouble you, but...?
That's all very well for you, but...?
Anything you want is OK with me.
I don't mind.
I don't know.
I'm sure you know better, but...
This is probably going to be an awful bother, but...
There was nothing I could do.
Are you very angry with me?
I'm really embarrassed to ask you this. but...
I'm not explaining myself very well, or, I'm probably not making
myself clear.
I'm useless.
Are you sure?
I don't mean to upset you.
Is it all right if I ask you a question?

It's all my fault, or, It must be my fault.

Is there anything else you need from me? or, Is there anything else I can do for you?

You can say no if you don't want to…

Please don't be upset.

I don't mean to be rude.

It's expected of me.

If you're sure it's all right, or, If that's OK with you.

I really need to ask you something.

Shall we?

What do you think?

Can I interrupt you?

I feel really awful, but…

No one ever listens to what I say, anyway.

It's all right.

Are you really sure you want to?

Don't blame me.

I'm hopeless at…

Sometime when it suits you, could you…?

Do you think it would be at all possible for you to…?

Could you do me a huge favour?

Unless you have any objections.

My opinions aren't worth much.

I'll make it up to you.

Excuse me, is it all right if I disturb you? or, I'm sorry to disturb you.

If no one else will do it, I guess I'll have to.

With all due respect…

When you have time…

As you become more conscious of what comes out of your mouth, add anything we've left off to the list.

We've been asked time and time again if what we have labelled as extraneous padding isn't oiling the wheels of good social intercourse. Yes, of course it is … some of the time. We're not suggesting that getting rid of all the fluff is the right thing to do. However, we think even asking the question about oiling the wheels is what a nice person might say who wants to justify their use of apology.

None of it is wrong. It is when it is used continually and thought-lessly, and as a way to hedge your bets, justify your behaviour, make excuses for yourself and otherwise avoid being direct and straightfor-ward that it is problematic. The words are simply words. It's how and why you use them that is the issue here not whether you *should never* say 'I'm sorry' ever again.

When you apologise, you need to be clear about what you are sorry for. Are you sorry for your actions or are you sorry for your person. If you're sorry for what you've done wrong, yes, apologise. If you're sorry for who you are, no, apology simply reinforces your low self-esteem.

For nice people the language of apology and the need to ask per-mission is habitual. That is what we aim to have you change; not the politeness or the gentlemanly or ladylike use of language that eases social interaction. We're all for good manners, but self-deprecation, dis-claimers and excessive apology are not good manners.

There is a little humorous aspect of over-apology that we are sure you must have encountered at some point. When there's so much apology thrown at the other person, *they* begin to apologise back and start tak-ing care of you. It can become almost farce-like and can go on for ever.

> You: 'I'm so sorry. I'm really very, very sorry.'
> Them: 'No, that's all right. I don't mind, really.'
> You: 'No, no, I'm just so ashamed. You'll never forgive me.'
> Them: 'There's nothing to forgive. I'm sorry you're so upset.'
> You: 'I'll make it up to you.'
> Them: 'Please don't be so upset, it's all right. I'm more sorry than you are.'

And then they strangle you!

One of our more interesting experiences in leading our workshops is having people attend for whom English is not their first language. This part of the workshop – the exploration of language – is a revela-tion to them because in learning English they didn't necessarily learn the padding that we take for granted. They may have it in their own language, but it's missing in their English.

It's why we think that some foreign people may sound abrupt or even rude to English ears – they haven't learned to oil their speech with words and phrases that take the edge off being straightforward. They don't have the social cotton wool that we've been brought up with.

The one exception was a lovely woman from France who is multi-lingual and who told us that every time she learns a new language it's the 'nice' words she tries to learn first: she seeks out the extraneous bits of apology so that she's sure to have them in whatever language she is speaking!

Little rules of behaviour you heard when growing up

Every family has rules (not all of them detrimental). In every family, someone in authority (or a number of someones) decides how every-one else in the family should behave. The axioms and sayings that you heard and absorbed when growing up will be the machinery that rein-forces the rules.

If you don't have anything nice to say, don't say anything at all.
Don't make a fuss.
Nice girls don't…
Little boys don't cry.
Be a man.
Be nice.
Children should be seen and not heard.
I'll give you something to cry about.
It's not worth the trouble.
I want doesn't get.
I know what you're thinking.
What's the magic word? (please, thank you, may I)
Go to your room.
Just wait till your father gets home.
I wouldn't do that if I were you.
Play nicely.
Manners maketh the man.
When I was your age…, or, In my day…

Think of the starving children in _____ (country of choice depending which generation you are part of).

You're breaking your mother's heart.

Take it like a man.

Give them the benefit of the doubt.

Don't come running to me when it all goes wrong.

If wishes were horses, beggars would ride.

You have to share.

I can't imagine what _____ would say if they were alive now, or, I'm glad _____ isn't alive to see you now.

I don't know why we ever had children in the first place.

You ought to be grateful, or, You're so ungrateful.

At least you have...

You don't know what it's like.

Don't spill the milk/drop the plate, etc.

I won't love you any more.

Why can't you be more like...?

Stop being so sensitive.

You don't want that.

How can you be so selfish?

Don't tell your father (mother).

We don't talk like that in this family.

FHB (Family Hold Back: in other words, guests get first choice).

I'll wash your mouth out with soap.

Cheer up.

You're just like your (father, mother, grandfather/mother, etc).

If you make a face and the wind changes, it will stay like that.

Always put other people first.

You'll understand when you have children of your own.

Father Christmas isn't going to come this year.

It's sure to end in tears.

You've brought such shame on this family.

You're such a baby.

We'll see, or, Maybe later.

You're all right.

You're such a disappointment.

Mark my words.

We'll send you away to a home/Borstal if you don't stop right now.
What will the neighbours think?
I've had enough of your nonsense.
Can't you stop thinking of any one but yourself for once?
I'm going to leave you if you don't start behaving yourself.
How could you do this to us?
Act your age.
You never were the brains of the family.
Least said soonest mended.
You're not leaving this house looking like that.
I didn't raise my children to behave like this.
Who do you think you are?
You don't want to get a swelled head, do you?
You'll understand when you grow up.
Is this all the thanks I get?
There's nothing to be afraid of.
You'll be the death of me.
Calm down, what are you getting so excited about?
I'm so ashamed of you, I'll never be able to hold my head up in public again.
For goodness' sake, grow up!
Don't be a show off.
You've made your bed, now you'll have to lie in it.

Around this point in the workshop, participants who are parents are saying, 'Oh my God, I've said the same things to my own children.' You may be aware that you say a lot of these things to your children, too. They're easy to say – they seem to come out of nowhere; they really come out of your subconscious storehouse of things that were once said to you. They're short cuts to get a child to stop doing whatever it is that you don't like and get it to do what you want it to do.

Add anything to that list we may have left off that was particular to your family. It may help to go back a generation to your grandparents who will have had some strong Victorian family behavioural strictures that have been passed down.

We've left out an entire area when we compiled the list, and that's the one of religion. If you were brought up with a strong religious base, there will probably be many things that were said to you to reinforce the teachings that were laid down by that religion.

You'll have been given rules about the way you are supposed to behave in the sight of God, Allah, Krishna, Jehovah or your particular deity. Connected to any religious upbringing you had (and which you may still be practising) will be moral teachings and guidelines of goodliness and godliness.

Whether you went to a church, synagogue, mosque, temple, ashram, zendo, meditation hall, etc, religion has very strong imperatives about the way you should live your life. You may want to include those in your list as well. They will be sayings, lessons, precepts, injunctions and principles taught to you as a child.

Have you ever been in a relationship where there was a clash of rules? Or did your parents have opposing sets of rules? In this situation, one person's 'truths' of acceptable, expected behaviour are different from the other's set of 'truths', etc. Who's right, then?

It's a bit like seeing the world through rose-tinted spectacles: your rules will be deeply embedded in your belief system, just as much as someone else's are in theirs. With two opposing systems under the same roof you can really see language at war. For children this can be doubly confusing. There is not only a conflict between what they feel inside and what they are hearing outside, but they might also be hearing diametrically opposed versions of the truth.

Cultural reinforcement

These are nursery rhymes and verses that from a very early age tell you what the world is like and how you're supposed to behave; they tell you that this is the way the world is supposed to be. They shape your morality and teach you valuable social lessons.

> *Sugar and spice and all things nice,*
> *That's what little girls are made of.*
> *Slugs and snails and puppy dogs tails,*
> *That's what little boys are made of.*

Seems harmless enough, but it makes sure you get the message that little girls and little boys are different in conventional and clearly defined ways. Hard if you're a little girl who likes slugs or a little boy who fancies being sugar and spice.

> *There was a little girl, who had a little curl*
> *Right in the middle of her forehead.*
> *And when she was good, she was very, very good.*
> *But when she was bad she was horrid.*

Let's get the two ends of the spectrum in one fell swoop – no middle ground for this little girl. If, like many little children, you were compared to this poor mite, you haven't been given much room to manoeuvre – you're either the bee's knees or you're wicked.

> *Georgie Porgie pudding and pie*
> *Kissed the girls and made them cry.*
> *When the boys came out to play*
> *Georgie Porgie ran away.*

So boys kissing girls isn't such a good thing, huh? Makes them cry. And of course, as soon as his mates come on the scene, he's off, leaving them to their tears.

> *Jack Sprat could eat no fat*
> *His wife could eat no lean*
> *And so betwixt the two of them*
> *They kept the platter clean.*

> *Rock-a-bye baby, in the tree tops*
> *When the wind blows, the cradle will rock*
> *When the bough breaks, the cradle will fall*
> *Down will come baby, cradle and all.*

> *Little Miss Muffet sat on a tuffet*
> *Eating her curds and whey*
> *Along came a spider and sat down beside her,*
> *And frightened Miss Muffet away.*

Dunce, dunce, double D
Cannot learn his ABC
Put the cap on
Then you'll see
What a silly boy is he
Dunce, dunce, double D.

There was an old woman
Who lived in a shoe
She had so many children
She didn't know what to do
She gave them some broth
Without any bread
Whipped them all soundly
And put them to bed.

All these rhymes are desired to give simple moral lessons, reaffirm beliefs about boys, girls, bodies, creepy-crawly creatures, stupidity and who knows what else.

Robin: I have a particular favourite (if that's the right term) axiom which seriously affected my life till I was about 30.

When I was seven there was a girl in my class who teased me unmercifully, until one day I couldn't take it any more and I hit her. Later, I was made to stand up in front of the whole class and was told in no uncertain terms by my teacher that:

Sticks and stones will break my bones
But words will never hurt me

In that moment one perfectly good and useful piece of socialisation got mixed up with one that's a lie. I shouldn't hit people, especially not girls. That's an important lesson and in my shame and humiliation at having done something I knew I shouldn't have, I took it on board lock, stock and barrel. I never hit anybody again.

There was just one problem. I took the second half of the lesson on board just as completely, and the second half of the lesson just isn't true. Words do hurt. As we have been emphasising throughout this chapter, words are powerful – they can hurt a lot. Yet I proceeded to go through life as though I was immune to anything that anyone said.

Until relatively recently I effectively numbed myself to any pain I experienced when people were horrid to me. Of course I was being hurt; I just believed and therefore behaved as if I wasn't.

But that little rhyme is chanted in playgrounds and classrooms everywhere, teaching a confusing mixed message that not all children can figure out.

We've given you a few rhymes here that we can remember just to get your mind going. What about you; are there any rhymes or songs that you can remember that had an effect on you? Even if you can't remember a specific effect, such as that which Robin experienced, think of any rhymes that stick in your mind. Then see what the underlying message is and what lesson a little mind is supposed to get from it.

What spontaneity?

Having looked through those lists and perhaps made some additions of your own, it's probably a little clearer now how language can have had such an impact in shaping your life. Words can undermine and wound your self-esteem quite badly. The biting, cutting and sometimes unthinkingly cruel things that were said to you will have contributed in a significant way to diminishing your self-esteem.

Language used like this kills your spontaneity. The things that were said to you over and over become the rules by which you are supposed to live your life. Because you absorbed them very early on, you have a little (or perhaps quite a large) rule book in your head which tells you what you are and are not supposed to do. That definitely gets in the way of being spontaneous and impulsive.

Lack of spontaneity means that every eventuality has to be thought of, every worry has to be gone over, every possibility has to be analysed.

You will be concerned about the outcome of every action; you will torment yourself with 'What if...'

'What if...' takes up an enormous amount of brain space, time and energy. The need to follow every strand of every possible outcome, of having to think through every eventuality, is an exhausting process. All the while you are concerned about what might happen, you are not paying attention to what is happening in the present (another useful coping mechanism when you were young; not so useful now).

You take your eye off the ball if you take your eye off the present. If you are not in the present but on some tortuous journey of 'this might happen and then that might happen and then this...' then you are certainly very far from being spontaneous and very locked into obeying the rules.

All these rules put limits on what you will allow yourself to do. They keep you narrow and small and prevent you from stepping outside the bounds of acceptable, good behaviour. They were laid down when you were little and you haven't forgotten them even if you can't remember them. They're there in your mind providing a running commentary on how you're doing.

Picture **yourself** at work in a meeting. One part of you will be present doing whatever it is you do, while your mind might be doing this: 'I'd better keep my mouth shut, my idea is pretty useless. I can't afford to make a fool of myself. I wonder what they think of me. I bet they don't even know I'm alive. Now if I do decide to speak I'd better be damn sure I know what I'm talking about or they'll shoot me down.' And so on and so on. You know what we're talking about.

Everyone has conversations in their head – it's impossible not to. But nice people tend to have conversations where they always come out last. When was the last time you really praised yourself for something you'd done? Not done well, or perfectly, or better than anyone else. Just done. Such as 'Isn't that great, I just cooked breakfast for the whole family again. Aren't I good?' or 'I'm really proud of myself, I spent the last hour photocopying these reports.'

Many of us, indeed, say critical things out loud!

Robin: 'Whenever I've done something not very clever (or what I think is not very clever), "stupid boy" comes out of my own mouth to tell me off!'

No, most likely you have to accomplish things and they have to be important to be worthy of praise. And of course, that praise has to come from someone else, and you might then self-deprecatingly demur. Learning to pat yourself on the back will be a great challenge and will fly in the face of all those codes and regulations that currently govern your behaviour and your speech.

Rules are reinforced over and over and over again in the language you use, the way you respond to other people, the way people respond to you and the endless chat that goes on in your head. The lists we've created are not supportive in the best sense of the word. What they do is support the worst feelings and thoughts you have about yourself, not the best.

Because these rules were given to you so young and are now so persuasive, they lie in your unconscious; you don't think about them. We suggested that developing your awareness of the language which you use is a major step in being able to change your behaviour. Becoming conscious about what you say and what you think is another.

It's the little things that count

We encourage you to start noticing your language. Since the art of saying no is very much bound up with language, this is a great place to start. First, your internal language: the easiest place to begin is with the endless talk you have up in your head. This is another situation where you'll be the only one who knows you're making any changes and it doesn't require you to speak anything out loud.

The next time you hear yourself give yourself a hard time, go back and thank your mind, but tell it that it would be more helpful if it gave you some praise, eg 'Thank you, Robin, for telling yourself you're so stupid, but I think it would be a better idea to give yourself three Brownie points for trying.' Don't tell it off for telling you off because then you perpetuate the whole cycle. Just a gentle nudge in the direction of complimenting yourself rather than heaping scorn on whatever it is you've just done.

Play the game of noticing every time you give yourself a hard time, 'Oh look, I've just told myself off. Why don't I retract that and start again.' NOT 'Oh you idiot, you've told yourself off again. What a wimp.'

The next step is to notice what comes out of your mouth. Not to change it, just to notice. You're unlikely to be able to change it right away, but if you can notice for yourself when these phrases plop out of your mouth, you are well on the way to altering some of your deeply entrenched verbal habits.

Noticing yourself saying 'I'm sorry' or 'Would you mind awfully…' counts as a win. When you suddenly become aware that you've used apology yet again, rather than chiding yourself for letting it happen, see if you can give yourself a tick for having been aware enough to notice it. Congratulate yourself on your new awareness rather than giving yourself a hard time for not changing.

'Look at that I just said I'm sorry again.' NOT 'You're pathetic, can't you pay attention and get it right?' You're noting and observing, not judging. You can begin to look on this as 'awareness after the fact'; a kind of game where you tally up the apologies and verbal padding you use during the day.

You can even do it more! As soon as an apology falls out of your mouth, notice out loud, exaggerate it or retract it. Thought after the fact is effective. Even if it happens minutes, hours, days or weeks later, the fact that you have brought something from your unconscious to your conscious is a win. The noticing is a change; the change is a win.

If you can begin to liberate yourself from the mocking, critical voice in your head and applaud yourself for noticing it in the first place, you build up your collection of wins.

When you're ready the next step might be to catch it during the fact, which might sound something like this: 'I'm sorry. Well, no, actually I'm not.' or 'I'm sorry. Now, wait a minute. Am I sorry?' Great you caught it. Great that you noticed it as it was coming out of your mouth and then you did something to change it. You could even apologise for apologising. 'I'm sorry. I'm sorry for saying I'm sorry, I didn't really mean to.' Again, any change is a win.

There's another little game you can play that requires almost no change whatsoever, but can make a huge difference in how you use the verbal padding. For instance, if you use the phrase, 'Is it all right if I ask you a question?' you are asking permission and giving the other person the absolute right to refuse. It's unlikely that's going to happen, but still, by asking permission you not only open yourself up to refusal, but you can also trigger the exasperation of the other person who might say, 'Why can't you just ask straight out?'

Try this. Instead of 'Is it all right ... etc.' alter just a few words so that it sounds something like this, 'I have a question for you' or 'Here's a question'. It may not look like that much of a change, but if you try it, you'll notice that it isn't obsequious or inviting refusal. It's more dynamic and active. It's still padding, but you are making a statement of intent.

Go down the list of your most common apologies and permission seeking questions and see what little adjustments you could make to change around the sense of them. It's a bit like fine-tuning your language. You don't need to change all of it, you simply need to tweak it here and there to fit more closely with what you really want to say.

All of this is to help you move from doing something automatically to doing something with thought. If you do enough of this and accumulate enough small wins, you will find that you won't be using the language of apology nearly so much. You won't be able to – it will begin to sound alien on your tongue.

6

A Boundary Is Not A Barrier

Stay on your side of the line, please

What is a boundary? A boundary separates one area from another. It's a line on a map that divides the end of your property and the beginning of the one next door; it indicates where one country/county/town ends and the next begins. A boundary separates one place from another place.

In general, we think of a boundary as something tangible that can be seen, such as a fence separating property or passport control separating countries.

The art of saying no is all about setting boundaries. As we said at the beginning of the book and will emphasise more than once, you may never actually use the word 'no'. The art is in how you present your wants and needs to other people. That's where boundary setting comes in. The boundaries we're now talking about are the ones that set the parameters of expected behaviour. For example: Little Johnnie comes running into your newly scrubbed kitchen with muddy trainers and you yell, 'Out of here this instant and take your shoes off before you walk on my nice clean floor!' You've set a boundary: Johnnie can come into the kitchen but only if he takes off his shoes.

At work you need peace and quiet whenever you have to prepare a report, so you tell the people in your department that you have an open-door policy except when the door is closed – then they can't disturb you. You've set a boundary: people are free to interrupt if your door is open, they can't if it's closed.

In each case the words effectively act as a dividing line, separating one kind of behaviour from another; the behaviour you want from other people.

Therefore, for the purposes of this book, we're going to define a boundary as anything that sets the limits of how far you choose to allow another person to come into your physical or emotional territory.

If the fear of consequences is the most inhibiting factor that stops you from conducting your life as you would like, then the inability to set effective boundaries is the manifestation of that fear.

External boundaries

The first area we're going to examine is that of physical or external boundaries. The clearest example of an external boundary is what is known as a Personal Space Boundary. This is the area that's approximately 18 inches from your body. It is called personal space because it feels like an extension of your very person. It's as though your body has an additional unseen part to it that reacts to the proximity of other people. In some beliefs, this personal space is called an aura.

If someone enters that space without your express consent, you will feel uncomfortable. Everyone has examples of someone entering their personal space uninvited: it feels awful. Overly nice people will have lots of examples of when someone crowded in on them, and they didn't like it but they didn't say anything. You know when your personal space boundary has been breached.

Now, because the kind of boundaries we are talking about aren't tangible, they are also moveable. Our personal space boundary is retracting and expanding all the time.

For instance, if you travel on public transport you will unconsciously draw your personal space boundary right up close to your body and generally 'leave the premises' by staring at the floor, reading a book or a newspaper or the ads, anything other than stare into the face of a complete stranger who is packed right up against you in rush hour. This drawing in of boundaries is a tacit, if uncomfortable, agreement by everyone travelling which enables a lot of people to get from one place to another relatively quickly.

The other places where you will automatically draw in your personal space boundary are in the cinema or theatre or at a concert. In those instances, you are putting yourself in quite a confined spaced often sitting right next to people you don't know so that you can all have the experience of that particular entertainment.

So that you won't be too disturbed by how close you are to someone you don't know in these circumstances, you will 'leave the premises' by focusing your attention on the screen or stage. You might even have a little silent skirmish with your neighbour to see who first puts their elbow on the armrest as a way to create some additional personal space in cramped conditions.

There will be other places particular to you where you draw in your personal space without thinking about it at all: at parties, in cramped working conditions, or when shopping in a crowded store at Christmas time. In each case, no matter how close you pull in the boundary, there is still a point beyond which it isn't all right for someone to go. That boundary is to protect you from an invasion of your territory.

When you extend your personal space boundary, you are putting more distance between you and other people. Most of you will have had a day (or two or three) when you didn't want anyone to come within five feet of you because you felt grumpy or fragile, were hung over or ill or simply wanted to be left alone. In some ways it's as though your skin takes on extra sensitivity to other people's vibrations and you can't bear them to be near you.

People in some countries (in the Middle East, for instance) have a closer personal space boundary than others, and cultural clashes often occur when there are dissimilar boundaries. For instance, it is sometimes a bit of a farce to see Western businessmen unconsciously moving backwards to create more space as Middle-Eastern businessmen unconsciously move towards them to create less.

The invasion of your personal space boundary can feel extremely unpleasant and can cause a great deal of anxiety. This kind of situation is a good example of when being too nice puts you into an emotionally compromised place. You want to be able to say 'Move!' but feel completely unable to do so.

When was the last time someone invaded your personal space without your permission? What did it feel like? More importantly, what did you do? Did you endure? If you endured it, what were your thoughts? Did you wish they would see how uncomfortable you were and move away? Did you imagine that they were doing it on purpose? Did you think they would be upset or offended if you told them to move away; or did you imagine they might get very angry if you said you didn't like them being so close?

If you did tell the other person to move or that you were uncomfortable, did they stop and move away? How did you tell them? Did you shove them, or were you able to tell them you didn't like them being so close? What happened then?

Did you try to compromise and simply move away yourself? Back off and hope the other person got the hint. Did they?

Protecting or defending a personal space boundary means you have to start being less nice and more direct. It's no good hoping people will get the hint, because most of the time they don't. They don't necessarily see that there's anything wrong.

Again, go back to the image of nice-tinted spectacles. You may find it hard to imagine that other people don't respect your space the way you respect theirs. You may be appalled that someone would just barge in and reach over you to pluck something off your desk without asking because you wouldn't dream of doing it to them.

Or you couldn't imagine going up to someone you didn't know very well and putting your arm around them and giving them a squeeze. A lot of people do that and don't see that there's anything wrong with it. And there isn't. Nor is it wrong to want them *not* to do it.

The difficulty is in wanting them not to do it but not saying anything about it. You may be cringing inside because you hate the squeeze, or the arm that shoots under your nose to reach for something, or someone standing too close to you at a party. But if you don't say anything they will just continue because you've given your unspoken permission to do so by not saying anything. You've agreed to their interpretation of the boundary.

Ah, but what if you *think* you've set a boundary? What if you have actually said to someone, 'Please don't do that' and they still walk all over you? What then?

There are a couple of issues here. First, there are the mixed messages that your body language maybe giving. You may be saying 'Please don't'

but if your body is giving a different message, then the other person
will not take you seriously.

Here are some techniques that we have found which help a great deal
when attempting to set a personal space boundary:

Not smiling

Smiling is a dead giveaway that you're trying to soften the message. It
gives carte blanche to someone who thinks you don't really mean it. If
you've got this big grin on your face they can tell themselves that really,
deep down, you like what they're doing.

Maintaining good eye contact

It is very hard for some of us to be able to look someone in the eye for
any length of time. Looking away tends to imply that you're not really
interested in pursuing the subject, but if someone can't see your face
clearly your words will carry far less weight.

Standing your ground

Backing off just doesn't work. It's wishy-washy. It gives no clear signal
of what your intentions are. The other person may not even realise
you're doing it, but will keep moving along with you so that they continually adjust the space to where they want it. Standing your ground
gives weight to your intention.

Speaking in a firm voice

Not necessarily loud, a common mistake. You don't have to yell to let
people know what you want, but the words do have to be firm and
strong to convey that you really mean it.

Telling the other person how you feel

This is letting the other person know you aren't comfortable with them
being so close. This can be difficult because it means revealing how
you feel and may make you feel very vulnerable. However, it is the
clearest way to let someone know that they are stepping over the mark
– your mark.

Not rising to the bait

You can get suckered into having conversations you don't want to have because you try to reason with the other person. Then the other person can dangle a seemingly irrefutable argument in front of you and you're hooked. If you don't want someone near you, you don't want them near you.

Agreement

If someone tells you you're being silly, agree with them; they have no place to go after that. 'You're being a bit touchy, aren't you?' 'Yes, you're right, I am.'

Exactly who is a boundary for?

Another issue is that we think just saying how we feel and what we want ought to do the trick. Even if you've got all the body language working in your favour – good eye contact, strong body signals, firm voice – some people still won't take the hint. What if you do all the things we've just suggested and it still makes no difference?

A boundary is not exclusively for you. It may seem as though it is because, after all, you're the one who's decided just how far you want someone to go and no farther. All well and good. But if you don't transmit that information to the other person so that it's really clear to them, all the wanting isn't going to do you any good.

A boundary is set for the other person's benefit as well as your own. A boundary is not effectively set until the other person respects and honours it.

A boundary, however, is not a barrier that is never to be breached. It is more like a border negotiated by two parties through which some people will be refused entry, or refused entry sometimes. This also means that 'conditions' of entry or refusal need to be 'published' clearly for the other person to see. It is your responsibility to let the other person know what you want or don't want from them: it is not their responsibility to be able to read your mind or interpret your signals of unease.

Some people will honour a boundary no matter how weakly you set it. They need very little prompting to get the message that you don't like whatever it is they're doing.

Others won't notice you until you're out there with two-inch planks, hammer and nails and a 'Keep Out' sign tacked on. That might mean that you will have to be more forceful in the way you let them know they have crossed a line and that you want them back on the other side. Until the other person sees it and respects it, your boundary isn't set.

Some people think repetition is setting an effective boundary and when that doesn't work, are perplexed: 'I told him over and over but he just wouldn't listen.' Repetition won't work unless you do something different to get your message across.

You might step out from the 'nice' end of the spectrum and move into the 'not nice' areas and find that nothing happens. 'Well, I took a risk and it didn't work.' At this point you may have to step even further into the not nice area and put more pressure on the other person in order that they get the message.

There are people who are so oblivious to the effect they are having on you that you need to do something dramatic to stop them trampling all over your boundary. This might mean moving all the way across the middle ground right up to the edge of being 'nasty'.

You might have to use phrases like, 'You're not listening to me' or 'What do I actually have to do to get you to pay attention?' or, 'If you don't stop that right now, I'm leaving.' You have to grab their attention for long enough so that they hear what you are saying.

If they won't hear that, then they are being abusive and you have every right to be nasty back to them.

We know of people who have quit their jobs rather than stand their ground and let the other person know the terrible effect that their behaviour was creating. We know people who won't go to parties any more because they always get saddled with the party bore and don't know how to get unstuck. They find it easier to avoid the party than to step into the Middle Ground.

There are some situations where the boundary setting is so poor that the problem gets magnified out of all proportion and can explode in everyone's face because it wasn't caught in time.

A great deal of sexual harassment does occur, particularly in the workplace. But our experience is that there are times when the 'offending party' has simply crossed a boundary that the 'offended party' thinks they've set but which has not been seen or acknowledged.

Here's a story we heard on one of our courses:

> Jane is a legal secretary who used to work for a very old, very conservative firm of solicitors in the City. Everyone was extremely polite and considerate and nothing ever seemed particularly hurried or urgent.
>
> Jane left London for Bristol and now works for a completely different kind of firm. Very young, very lively, with a group of solicitors who don't know a boundary from a budgerigar. In particular, one of the senior partners is very tactile and whenever he asks Jane into his office he moves from behind his desk to sit on the arm of her chair while he explains what he wants done. Jane hates this.
>
> At first, she just scrunched herself up as small as she could and leaned away from him. He didn't notice. She complained to friends that she thought he was trying to rub up against her.
>
> Then she tried to make a joke of it and while giggling, she told him that he'd better be careful or she'd tell his wife. That didn't work, he didn't know what she was talking about.
>
> Then she took to standing up when she came in, refusing to sit down, she was pressed for time. He simply came and stood next to her and put his arm around her shoulders.
>
> Jane was now in a real state. She was sure he was deliberately making sexual advances and she now told other colleagues that he was harassing her.

It was only after doing one of our workshops that she tried some of the more forceful boundary setting techniques to see if she could stop the man. She rang us shortly afterwards to let us know that in the end it took very little. Actually, it took a lot of courage and bravery for Jane to have all the fearful feelings she was experiencing (the main one being that if she confronted him, she'd lose her job) and still attempt to set clear, unambiguous boundaries with this man.

She told us that the next time he draped his arm around her, she gently removed it and, looking him in the eyes, told him that she didn't like it when he got too close. Apparently he was astonished and told her that no one else complained, so why hadn't she said something sooner. Jane said that she almost got cold feet then because he had a point, but she stood her ground and reiterated that she didn't like it and that she was complaining now.

He stopped. She didn't get fired. And she didn't have to charge him openly with sexual harassment either, which could easily have happened.

Let's be clear that we *know* that a lot of sexual abuse does happen, but as we can see in Jane's story, it is very easy for a situation to get out of hand because there is such a weak boundary that it is neither seen nor honoured.

The other person doesn't know there's anything wrong. But you think they ought to know! How? You have to tell them.

What if it's real?

If you genuinely know that someone is harassing you, sexually or otherwise, then boundary setting is particularly important. If you do not set a boundary that the 'abuser' can see, then you are giving your tacit approval that what the other person is doing is all right with you.

Even if they *know* it isn't all right with you, they can convince themselves that you really don't mind.

We know that some people are afraid of saying anything because the other person can deny that there ever was deliberate sexual harassment and may even cause an embarrassing scene.

Going and talking about it to other people isn't going to stop someone from getting at you, unless the 'other people' are willing to intervene on your behalf.

This is how you could deal with such a situation:

> You: 'I don't like your behaviour towards me; I'm offended and feel demeaned when you make sexual comments in front of me.'
>
> The Other Person: 'Are you accusing me of something?'
>
> You: 'Yes, I think you're harassing me and I don't like it. I want you to stop.'
>
> TOP: 'I haven't done anything wrong. I think you're just looking for trouble.'

> You: 'I'm not going to get into an argument with you. I want you to stop making offensive comments when you're with me.'

People who harass others usually pick people they think won't fight back. Getting your position clear as soon as the first incident occurs will save you a lot of grief and heartache in the future.

More dire consequences

Sometimes the things we fear most do happen.

> **Jo Ellen:** I was standing in a queue at the local Post Office where two windows were operating. When it was my turn I went up to one of the windows and noticed that someone was standing really close behind me – too close for comfort.
>
> In those split seconds that seem like minutes I handed over my transaction and thought about the person breathing down my neck: I didn't like it. Should I endure? That's what I would have done in the past: after all it's just a few minutes and he probably isn't doing it on purpose; I doubt he's really being a pervert. Maybe I should say something? But he might not like it and cause a scene. No, he won't do that, not in a Post Office.
>
> First step was compromise. I turned around and glared at him. That had absolutely no effect on him whatsoever. 'Oh well,' I thought, 'I really don't like this, I'm going to have to say something.' So I did.
>
> 'Would you mind moving move back a bit; I'm really uncomfortable with you standing so close.'
>
> What did he do? He caused an almighty scene! We said earlier that stepping into the Middle Ground even a little bit can trigger someone else's nastiness. Well, I triggered his. He went bananas! He carried on, trying to enlist the sympathy of the rest of the queue (who were pretending they were somewhere else) in his cause of making me out to be a nutter.

He shouted that I was sick and, having realised that I had unknowingly created a monster, I used the agreement technique, saying, 'You're right, I am sick, which is why you need to stand away from me.' He continued ranting till he got to the window, handed over his benefits book and was told he couldn't have it back – there was something wrong with it. He then transferred his ranting to the postal worker; I got a reprieve, finished my business feeling vindicated and left.

I couldn't have known what was going to happen. When we set boundaries, we don't know what the outcome is going to be. You can't know.

However, just because every once in a while the worst does happen, that is no reason not to set boundaries when we feel our space is being infringed upon.

Beyond personal space

Sometimes physical boundaries need to be set that stretch out way beyond your personal space.

These are the situations where something that belongs to you, or perhaps your time is considered fair game by others. This could be people who overstay their welcome, establishing themselves in your home or at your dinner table, comfortably settling in for a long period. It could be a friend who rings you up at the most inconvenient times to bend your ear and is impervious to your subtle hints that you have other things to do.

There are flatmates who borrow your clothes without asking and neighbours who wander around your home and perhaps head straight for the fridge to see what goodies you have. There are colleagues who pick up papers from your desk and read them in the comfort of your chair.

There are parents who don't recognise that there is any separation at all between you and them and treat your home, your friends, your aspirations as their own.

Here are two stories that highlight these boundary issues:

Samantha's story: Samantha is a very generous, warm-hearted person. She likes entertaining and because she and her husband are financially comfortable, they have a large London flat and a house in the country. People come to visit: for a day, a weekend, a week. She likes being a hostess.

In general, Samantha is a very self-confident, self-assured person. But she had one area where her boundary setting was non-existent. This was where Samantha's niceness got her into trouble: she didn't know how to tell people when it was time to leave (or rather, when she wanted them to leave).

It came to a head one weekend when friends appeared who she thought were only going to stay for that weekend. They ended up staying for a week. Samantha and her husband felt trapped. They hid in their bedroom much of the time and contrived excuses to be out of the house. They complained to each other about their over-staying house guests and how awful it was. But they never said anything to their guests. These friends never knew they were being considered a burden; they never knew how angry their hosts were getting.

Samantha was definitely being too nice. She felt that if she said something to them, they would feel offended and rejected and that would end their friendship. Meanwhile, the friendship was rapidly going sour anyway because of how Samantha was feeling about them: 'I'll never invite these two again, even for a day!'

Samantha had to become clear about how to set some simple boundaries without upsetting anyone: herself or her friends. For her it was a matter of having a little questionnaire in her head that she could go through with her friends before they arrived.

Things are different now. When Samantha invites people to visit she knows exactly when they are arriving and, more importantly, exactly when they are leaving. She is able to say what's inconvenient for her, rather than trying to second-guess what might be convenient for her guests.

We even heard from Samantha recently as we were writing this book. She was delighted that when one of her cousins rang her recently and invited herself to stay for a week, first, she was able to set a boundary by telling her cousin she couldn't make a decision right away. Then, having thought about it, she decided she didn't want any house guests, rang her back and set another boundary. She was able to say that it wouldn't really be convenient this summer but that she'd love to have her another time.

Paul's story: He was delighted when he moved into his own rented accommodation after leaving college. Finally, he could stay up as late as he wanted, have parties every weekend if it suited him and watch whatever took his fancy on the TV without asking anyone if it was all right. He quite fancied a bachelor's life for a while and a had a regular stream of mates dropping in after work and on the weekends.

He repairs photocopiers and thinks it's a great job. He counts himself lucky that he works for a firm that hasn't made any redundancies during the recession, so he feels pretty secure.

He doesn't feel so secure in his own flat, however. One or the other of his parents rings him every single day to find out how he is. At first they rang him at the same time every day, so he avoided answering the phone then. But they took to surprising him at different times, so that didn't work.

He feels about two years old sometimes. There he is, stretched out on the sitting room floor eating junk food and watching football when his parents tap on the door, saying they were just in the neighbourhood and decided to drop by. His mother then proceeds to clean up his mess, criticise his eating habits and unpack the groceries she bought, while his father chides him for not going after a promotion.

Once he was soaking in the bath recovering from a hard night out, when his parents knocked on the door. This time he pretended he couldn't hear and turned the bath taps on full in an effort to drown out the sound. They, however, were persistent. To his acute embarrassment his mother even yelled through the door that she knew he was in there and to let them in.

Which he did, dripping and hung-over. That gave them something to talk about: he shouldn't drink, he smokes too much and he shouldn't stay out late, he'll lose his job if he keeps this up.

He lost his temper, told them they were interfering in his life because they didn't have one of their own and banged into his bedroom, telling them to leave.

Paul's problem is hard. It's typical of the difficulties that parents and children have in separating from each other. Paul loves his parents and part of him is pleased with the groceries and the concern. Most of him isn't though. He wants to be a slob sometimes and drink his brains to mush. He feels he's responsible enough to know just how far to go and isn't jeopardising his job with a good night out.

His parents can't accept that Paul isn't their baby any more and can't let go of the control they're so used to wielding in their own home. They really are proud of him, but won't trust him to make, and learn from, his own mistakes. All they want is to protect him from the real world.

Paul had to learn how to set boundaries to protect himself and his parents from each other. He did not find it easy to tell them not to ring him every day and always to warn him when they were planning to drop by.

He had to set these boundaries many, many times. They'd work for a week or two and then his parents would slip back into dropping by unannounced and ringing daily.

Paul knew he had to keep making journeys into the Middle Ground because he really didn't want to flip over into Nasty the way he had done before. He had to let them know again and again that though he loved them they couldn't keep treating him like a little boy.

In most cases parents are the hardest to be 'not nice' to. But using some simple boundary setting as a start can help ease the separation without making either party wrong.

Interestingly enough, the hints and tips that we gave for protecting your personal space work just as well in these kind of situations. Strong voice, clear intention, not smiling, all contribute to conveying the message that you are serious.

Internal boundaries

Even if people ignore them, an external boundary is still obvious. It's clear to you when someone steps over the line and crosses into your personal space.

Internal boundaries, however, are different. **All internal boundaries relate to the things about you that no one can know about unless you tell them.**

Having a weak internal boundary is when the other person tramples all over something you are sensitive about and they never know they've done it because you haven't told them.

People have issues in their lives that they are particularly sensitive about. You will have yours. They could be anything, from hating the shape of your body to the fact that you are estranged from your sister, to the embarrassment you feel because of your acne or the shame you feel about being unemployed. Whatever yours are, it will be upsetting to you if someone inadvertently begins to chatter on about them expecting you to take part in the discussion.

It's not as though they are doing it on purpose. They have no idea about your sensitivity or how upset you get about these issues, and unless you tell them, will carry on as though nothing is wrong.

Let's say your mother is dying of cancer and you can't even bear to hear the word, let alone talk about it coherently. A friend comes along and tells you about the latest research into the effects of chemotherapy. Inside you are cringing and crying, but if you are being too nice, you will nod and smile and pretend that you are listening.

That's an example of an internal boundary that has been crossed without the other person even knowing that they've done it.

Meanwhile, you're in agony because you don't know how to protect yourself from this kind of invasion. If you continue to maintain silence or give vague hints that something may be wrong without telling the other person there is anything the matter, then you have a weak internal boundary.

Weak internal boundaries are the easiest to knock over. They can't be seen; they are very personal to you and while they are being trampled over, the nice you will be thinking of all kinds of reasons why you can't say anything.

Claire's issue is an example of what we are talking about: she is very sensitive about her weight. She considers herself too large and is torn between trying new diets and feeling that diets are a tyranny and ultimately unhealthy. She doesn't want to expose her feelings to anyone and would prefer not to talk about the issue at all.

Here's a typical conversation that Claire often finds herself in the middle of, where she is unable to set an effusive internal boundary – for instance with her friend Terry.

'Claire, I've just read about the most fantastic sounding diet. I'll make a copy for you.'

'That's all right, I'm not really into diets at the moment.'

'Well, my dear, you could afford to lose a few pounds you know.'

'I know, but I don't think diets are an especially good idea. I hate them and I get cranky and then I fall off the wagon and gain even more weight.'

'You're probably not going about it the right way. You have to exercise and change your lifestyle. Really, Claire, pull yourself together and stop making excuses.'

'I don't have time for exercise and I can't afford a gym anyway.'

'You don't need to go to a gym. Listen, I think it would be a great idea if we met three mornings a week before work and did some yoga. I'm sure I could get a couple of the other girls to join in. It'll be fun.'

'I don't know, Terry, I'll think about it.'

'Don't think about it. Just do it. Otherwise you'll keep putting it off and then all I'll hear about is how unhappy you are because you can't find any clothes that fit.'

'Well, maybe...'

And so on and so on. Claire has been stuck on this conversational wheel more than once. Like a hamster, going nowhere fast.

Claire goes through a whole range of nice behaviour here. First she hints that she doesn't want to get into the subject by saying she doesn't believe in diets, without ever telling Terry she doesn't want to talk about it. She gets defensive, she comes up with a collection of excuses, she prevaricates and finally she's about to give in.

When Claire brought this situation to The Nice Factor, this is the way the conversation was replayed, with Claire setting some very strong internal boundaries.

'Claire, I've just read about the most fantastic sounding diet. I'll make a copy for you.'

'No need to do that Terry, I'm not going on diets any more.'

'Well, my dear, you could afford to lose a few pounds, you know.'

'Terry, I don't want to talk about diets and I don't want to talk about my weight.'

'You're going to have to face it at some point, Claire, and I'm here to support you.'

'Terry, you're not listening to me. I don't want to talk about it.'

'Well, I think you're being over-sensitive. Not talking about your size isn't going to make it go away, you know.'

'You're right. I am sensitive about it and I'd really like it if you respected that and left it alone. Now, let's talk about something else. I hear Linda's got a dishy new bloke.'

'Hmm. All right. And yes, Linda's in love for the umpteenth time as usual.'

Claire set her internal boundary using a few simple techniques. First, after she realised the direction the conversation was going, she stated clearly and directly what she wanted, which was not to talk about it. Then she stated it again, getting her friend's attention by telling her she wasn't listening. She did not rise to the bait and finally she used agreement to take the wind out of Terry's sails and effectively to stop the way the discussion was going. She was able to steer the conversation away from dangerous ground without getting angry at Terry or feeling trapped by Terry's view of the situation.

That's why internal boundaries are often so hard to set. You may be afraid you will be exposing your vulnerabilities if you let other people know you are sensitive and don't want to talk about it. You may feel you have to justify yourself. You may feel you have to take care of the other person's feelings and go along with their suggestions so they don't feel bad.

Mostly, though, you are giving your power away to other people who can then control the direction of the conversation and steer it wherever they want it to go. It's as though a part of you feels that they have the *right* to push you into a corner and tell you how to live your life. If you have a weak internal boundary, you will be easy to push around. It's best not to have the conversation at all.

Poor internal boundaries are one of the main reasons why you may get so very angry inside. You get drawn into discussions you don't want to have, about topics you want to keep to yourself, hearing other people's views about what you ought to do. You don't like it. You don't want to talk about your weight, your mother's cancer, your unemployed status, your acne.

You don't want to hear about diets, miracle cures, dermabrasion or the best employment agency to go to. Yet, you'll find yourself spending time on the phone, during your lunch hour and over tea having conversations you simply don't want to have, and all because you feel you can't establish your 'conditions of entry' at your own internal border control.

There will be many places in your life where you have no problem whatsoever setting internal boundaries: you're probably not even aware you're doing it. It might be that you are brilliant at telling double glazing salespeople to go away, you're not interested. Or maybe you're good at not engaging with people who sell religion door-to-door. Or maybe you're particularly clever at not buying oven mitts and ironing board covers.

If you look, you will find that you have places where your border control is in firm command of the situation. It tends to become ineffective however, in those areas where you feel especially vulnerable.

Setting a firm internal boundary doesn't require you to have the right words, it doesn't require you to try to sort out anyone's problems. You don't have to be nasty or make the other person feel that they are wrong.

You don't have to be rude or aggressive. You don't have to go into lengthy explanations or try to convince the other person that you're right or defend your actions. You don't have to do any of the things that nice people are usually quite frightened of and are loath to do anyway.

The great thing about boundary setting is that it can be done with the minimum of words and the maximum of intention, using the same techniques we mentioned earlier in the chapter: maintaining eye contact, not smiling, holding your ground, not engaging with someone else's point of view and drawing the conversation to a close as quickly as possible.

All these techniques help you stay more in charge and less at the mercy of other people. They help relieve the pressure of carrying around all those feelings of helplessness and disharmony.

All the while there is a large discrepancy between your internal feelings and your external behaviour, you are operating with ineffective boundaries. Good boundaries bring the internal and the external you into closer alignment.

As with an external boundary, you are saying to the other person, 'You can go this far and no farther.'

7

Who's On Top?
Playing The Status Game

What's in a status symbol?

Status: rank, standing, hierarchy, pecking order, class, caste, position.

High status

Who are the highest status people you can think of? The Queen, the Pope, the Prime Minister, the President of the United States, your bank manager, your mother/father, your boss, Nelson Mandela, the Dalai Lama, the Sultan of Brunei, John Paul Getty, Madonna, Arnold Schwarzenegger, a policeman, Mohammed Ali, Pele, David Beckham, Mother Theresa?

Imagine defining status on a scale of one to ten, with ten being the highest. Who are the top scorers that come to mind?

Make a list of everyone that you think of as having high status.

How did they achieve that status? Were they born with it, as the Queen was? Do they have some power over you, as your bank manager, your boss or your parents have? Were they elected to high office, did they make a lot of money or become pop stars or movie stars? How do you know when someone has status?

Did they get it because they're people who stand up and fight hard for their beliefs, as Nelson Mandela and the Dalai Lama have done? Or do they have it because they have the power to give you points on your licence or arrest you?

What about professions that by their very nature have high status: doctors, barristers, college and university professors, Members of

Parliament, scientists, explorers, architects, painters, composers, writers – the list is endless.

How do **you** define status – as power, prestige, wealth, celebrity, charisma? The people you consider to have high status may be very different from the ones chosen by someone else. You may cower in your car if a policemen catches you speeding, making him very high status because of the power he has over you; while someone else will jovially try to talk themselves out of getting a summons because to them a policeman is just a regular bloke in a uniform.

You might get tongue-tied if you suddenly meet the head teacher of your child's school because he or she seems so powerful to you, while someone without children when seeing the same person just says hello to their neighbour.

Low status

What about low status? Who comes to mind when you think of the lowest status people you can imagine? Make a list of these people. This is the bottom of the barrel, the lowest of the low.

A person sleeping rough? A criminal serving a long prison sentence? The boy/girlfriend who treated you badly and who you now think is just scum? A dustman, a Member of Parliament, an estate agent, a dropout, someone on the dole? A person with a handicap? An unwed mother, a bankrupt? What about a person of a different ethnic or religious background?

Think of status on a scale of one to ten, with one being the lowest status a person can have. Who can you think of who's a 'one'? How do **you** define someone who has low status – because of their poverty, their profession, their education, their accent? Is it their body language, their low self-belief and self-esteem? Is it because you think you are better than they are? Does assigning low status to someone else play out your prejudices and beliefs?

Do you just assume that certain people have low status because they fit your picture of what a low-status person is?

As much as we might think otherwise, status is not owned by the other person. Status can only be conferred by us.

You make judgements about someone – whether they are famous or not – based on *your* criteria of what high or low status is. If money is very important to you, then people who earn a lot will have high status. If standing up for fundamental beliefs is important to you, then Nelson Mandela may be at the top of your list. If you are religious, the leader of your religion will hold a high position in your esteem.

Conversely, if money isn't a status symbol to you, how rich someone is won't make a bit of difference. If you think political activists are misguided idealists, no matter how famous someone is, you won't be in awe of them. And if you aren't religious, you won't see what all the fuss is about when the Pope makes a visit.

There are people who view themselves as having high status and expect to be treated with respect; but if enough people don't concur and confer that status on them, their expectations won't be realised. Then they come across as arrogant and snobbish.

In the same way, there are people who are so insecure and feel so bad about themselves that they imagine themselves to be wormy and unworthy. Yet other people will elevate them and give them a status that they themselves don't feel they deserve.

Your fear can elevate someone to high status, just as your contempt can lower someone.

Do we need it?

Why do we have status? Why can't everyone just be equal and go about their business? Sounds good in theory, but human nature is such that we need status. In a way, it's a form of security. We need to find our place in the pecking order; we need to make comparisons about who we are in relation to other people. We need measurements to define ourselves.

Our esteem is sometimes dependent on being better off or worse off than other people. Ideal though it may be to be content with ourselves and develop our own sense of self-worth without comparisons, it's well-nigh impossible to achieve that without having a list of criteria to measure ourselves against. You will have your set of criteria: academic achievements, salary, relationships, looks, sporting ability, sexual prowess, heritage, race, family history, religion, possessions, etc.

You can and do take your checklist out and start looking around and comparing yourself to others to see how well or how poorly you are doing. Meanwhile, everybody else is busy doing the same thing.

So what's all this got to do with being too nice?

Maintaining the status quo

While you are spending time comparing yourself with other people, attempting to see where you fit into the pecking order, you are reinforcing the idea of status: yours and theirs. When you assign someone a higher status than yours, you are, in essence, lowering your own status. In turn, if you look down on someone and give them a low-status rating, you are raising yours.

When you are being too nice, you confer a higher status on the people you are being too nice to. Every time you give in to someone else's arguments, you've made them more important than you. Every time you capitulate and swallow your tears, you have allowed the other person to have an ascendancy over you. Every time you accommodate or modify your behaviour or become someone you think other people want you to be, you have lowered your status and raised theirs.

You may think they are beneath contempt while you're doing it, no one else is going to know that except you (and the good friends you complain to).

By assigning a higher status to someone else, even if you don't want to, you are making yourself more burglarable. You are giving out the signals that you are low and therefore it's OK for them to behave as if you don't matter: if someone wants to out-status you, even unconsciously, they will.

By deferring, you make other people better than you. You are tacitly agreeing that they must be better or know more than you. Part of the reason you defer and give someone a higher status is because there are many times when you really *do* believe that they know better than you, so you've become used to deferring. The more you are used to it, the more you defer to other people's supposed higher status and the cycle goes on and on.

They're so clear and decisive they must have a better idea of the way things are supposed to be than you do. They are so definite and insistent that of course their opinion is worth more than yours. Even if your instincts are fighting against that information, there is a part of you that is so used to having your wants and needs defined by other people that they get the status and you don't.

People currently have a view of you. Some people may think you are a pushover and they take advantage of you whenever they get a chance. Others may see you as a generous, giving person who's always pleasant and has time to spare. Still others may see you as someone who has fierce temper tantrums and so they try to stay out of your way.

Your parents may still treat you as a ten-year-old. Your partner may see you as someone malleable and biddable; your colleagues may see you as insignificant; your best friend as someone who's 'got to learn to stand up for yourself for goodness' sake and stop getting walked on all the time'.

However you are viewed, if all your actions sustain those views then you are colluding in maintaining the status quo: the status quo that you and they have established.

The status quo is a difficult place to get out of: people are used to you as you are and you are used to being there. Your fears and anxieties make it difficult to create the momentum needed to change your behaviour. There is also a part of you that has become so used to your assigned status that it's become almost comfortable. The term 'comfortably uncomfortable' describes this state of being.

Maintaining the status quo is the unspoken agreement everyone has that things will stay the same. We use the word 'collude', because you are now party to preserving a balance that, however disagreeable, keeps things ticking over 'nicely', thank you very much. Given that most of the world wants you to stay the way you are – wants you to stay well entrenched in the agreed status quo – how could you use the very concept of status to turn things around for yourself?

The rest of this chapter is devoted to examining a whole range of what we hope you will find thoroughly enjoyable ways of tipping over the status quo and playing with status change as a way of becoming less nice.

We're going to be looking at status as a game, where not only are you the only player, but you have all the best shots.

A day in the life…

Status is changeable, status is always on the move.

In extreme cases you get a situation like Nelson Mandela's where, up until a few years ago, much of the world saw him as a low-status person who could rot in jail for all they cared. That's all changed now:

he is an elder statesman, courted by the very people who disdained him previously. That's certainly one way of looking at status change, albeit quite a dramatic one.

What about something a bit less dramatic. What about your change of status? In the last two pages it may have seemed that we were saying that you have one status and that's it. Not so.

It is true that everyone operates at a preferred status. There will be a status level at which you feel most comfortable and at which most people see you. This will be the status that you 'play' most of the time. You will, however, change your status many times during the day without even being aware you're doing so.

Status is a 'game' that you are playing every day of your life. There will be many times during the day when you will alter your behaviour depending on where you are, who you are with, what you are doing. This changing behaviour is governed by the way you view yourself and the way you view other people.

Let's look at this 'game' in more detail.

We'd like you to think about yesterday. Bring the entire day into your mind: all the things you did, places you went, people you spoke to. What were the interactions and how did they turn out?

Let's use a scale of one to ten to denote status level. Assign numbers to each of those transactions (I was a 'four' he was a 'nine'; I was an 'eight', she was a 'three', etc.). If you think about how you changed your behaviour during the day, you will see that you were continually changing your status to fit the situations. You will have been a 'seven' at one time and a 'three' at another, then back up to an 'eight' and down to a 'five'.

If you were trying to get the children dressed, fed and on their way to school was it smooth sailing or a screaming match? What status did you have to adopt to get them ready and out of the door? Maybe you don't have any children and the morning was a leisurely lie in and you had plenty of time to get yourself ready for your day. What did that feel like? Would that have been a 'ten' type of feeling?

Maybe you had to take the car into the garage: were you a two, deferring to their better knowledge, or did you act an eight so they wouldn't know you didn't know what you were talking about (or maybe you do)?

Maybe you were stuck on a train and were nervous about getting into work late. What did that do to your status? How did you act when you got to work? A grovelling, apologetic 'one'?

What if you had to go and sign on for the dole and stand in a long queue waiting for your turn: did that feel high or low? What number would you give for how it felt?

Maybe you went to the hairdresser or barber: what was your status there? A doctor or dentist's appointment: did you feel two years old and scared or was it an ordinary occurrence?

Did you have to see a solicitor about unpaid maintenance or an estate agent about buying a flat? Or maybe you had to borrow money from a friend. You may have had a long chat with one of your closest friends or an argument with someone on the other end of the phone.

In each of those situations you will have been behaving at a particular status level, without even thinking about it. You'll have known instinctively what tone of voice to use, what body language to display, what words to use or a particular attitude to adopt.

Indeed, did you think about changing your behaviour at all or did it come automatically? In most cases it will have come automatically. You will not have thought about what to do, you will just have done it. If you were too nice on occasion, even that will have been automatic.

If you use yesterday as a template, a kind of model of how you change your behaviour constantly depending on the circumstances, how did you actually do it? Well, you will have unconsciously assessed the situation and made a decision about how to behave: you will have, in essence, assigned a status number to yourself and other people and behaved accordingly.

Yes, there may be a preferred status which you used most of the time, but no matter what that status is, you will still have gone through a number of changes during your day.

Nobody ever stays the same status all the time – it's impossible. You might feel high status when giving instructions to your secretary, and low status when your mother calls to find out why you haven't phoned recently.

These changes of status are a major part of how you live your life. There will be situations where you defer and situations where you demand. There will be times when you capitulate and times when you stand your ground. There will be instances when you feel intimidated or manipulated and instances when you do the intimidating and manipulating. This behaviour has become so habitual that you're not aware of how much power you actually have to change the way you behave when you'd like to.

The capacity to change your behaviour *at will* is very much available to you.

Go over in your head those situations yesterday when you automatically altered your behaviour as a normal part of every day interaction with other people. There was no thought about it – it just was. You handed your money to the bus conductor, you went to the post office to send a package, you ran a meeting of department heads, you went to your classes at college, you picked up your dry-cleaning, you met a friend for lunch – all the while changing your status throughout the day.

Each time you will have made little adjustments in your behaviour; not necessarily massive ones, just the everyday modifications that makes your life smoother. These changes are so much a part of your built-in self that you're simply not aware of what you're doing. You changed your behaviour at will.

Now go over the day and see if there were any times when you changed your behaviour and wished you hadn't – where your too nice self adapted to a situation where you wanted to behave differently. Were there times when, looking back, you cringe a little in embarrassment because you believe you 'ought' to have done it one way and you ended up doing it the nice way instead? Were there things you wanted to say and didn't?

In these situations, too, you also changed your status at will, but because the fear of consequences may once again have got in the way, the status changes you made didn't feel much like choice. However, they were.

Playing the status game

We're now going to have you play a couple of versions of a little status game in the privacy of your own head.

The first version

Most likely you've been to buy food some time recently. Bring to mind the last time you took a trip to the supermarket. What was standing in the queue (if there was one) like? Did you just get on with your business, unload your trolley, pay for the groceries and leave? Did you chat with the person behind or in front of you or with the checkout clerk? Did you have any children with you who were bored and causing a fuss? Did you endure someone else's children who were being difficult?

Were you in a wheelchair or on crutches? Did you have to rely on someone else to go with you to carry your groceries for you? Were you in a terrible rush and impatient that things were taking so long, or was your trip the first time you'd been out that day so you were taking your time?

Using the one to ten analogy, see if you can imagine playing out that same scene as a 'ten', the top of the heap, the highest of the high. What would you do as a ten in the queue now? Would you be witty and charming, chatting to everyone around or would you be imperious and demanding? Would you toss your groceries on the counter or place them carefully to let everyone know you are taking all the time you need? Would you demand that someone packed your bags? See just how high-status you can imagine being and what that would look like.

Now, imagine the same scene played out as a 'one', the lowest of the low. Would it mean apologising a lot for taking up breathing space? Would it mean trying to be invisible and paying for everything as quickly as possible so you didn't take up anyone's time? Play with this; exaggerate what you imagine lowly behaviour to be. See just how silly you can be replaying your supermarket scene as a 'one'.

Could you imagine doing any of that in real life? What if you went some place where no one knew who you were? Could you imagine playing with changing status then, just to see what it would be like?

The second version

Now pick a situation from yesterday when you were too nice. If you actually managed to have a whole day when you weren't too nice, then pick the last time you found yourself maintaining the status quo when you didn't want to.

In each version we want you to completely over-exaggerate your behaviour. Over the top when you're high, over the top when your low. Take each version beyond the realms of reality. Create the sort of scene you might see in a Monty Python sketch and then double it! Have a fantasy about behaving in a way that you'd never conceive was possible.

As in the last version, first play the scene as a 'ten'. This is where you say everything that's in your head and more. This is where you stomp around and give the other person a piece of your mind. This is when you demand that things be done your way for a change. It's a time when you insist that other people change their behaviour to suit you. You can lord it over the other person and make their life miserable.

This is when you pull yourself up to your full height and pull rank (even if you don't have it). This is when you treat everything and everyone around you as objects of contempt, there purely for your convenience: include the furniture and especially other people.

Imagine losing your temper deliberately and saying whatever comes into your head even if it doesn't make any sense. You can tell the other person they really aren't good enough to be walked on because you wouldn't want to mess up your shoes. They are vile and insignificant and they should be fed to the crocodiles. Anything.

Or you can be utterly gracious in your 'ten-ness' so that they know exactly who's boss. You can deign to give them the time of day because, really, you are very grand and charitable. You can be a jolly good mate, all the while being just ever so slightly 'better than'. Smile a knowing smile. Look down on them. Patronise them.

Exaggerate this scene. Play with all the possibilities that could make you walk away from it feeling very ten indeed.

Now, imagine the entire scene played out with you as a 'one'. You grovel, cringe and apologise to such an extent that the other person is aghast at your behaviour. You may imagine being so obsequious that they want to kill you, you're so annoying. You beg and plead and cry and fling yourself on the ground.

In this version your whole body language slumps; you're self-pitying and terribly sad. You whine. You sigh a lot and wring your hands. You might imagine making yourself so invisible and talking in such a low voice no one can hear you.

Or you may try to win them over by being such a sugary, sweet, over-accommodating 'one' they don't quite know what's hit them. This is the 'sucking up' version of low status. This is when you fawn all over them, telling them how very, very wonderful they are and how disgustingly horrible you are.

How silly can you be as a 'one'? Can you get so low that you even embarrass yourself just thinking about it? How much fun can you imagine having being subservient and servile?

Now, this is not to say you should go marching out into the world putting these types of behaviour into practice. Our aim here is to let you imagine just what extremes of behaviour you are capable of, even if it's just in your head. Just as you altered your behaviour in little ways during your day yesterday, you have the capacity to alter your behaviour in very big, very extravagant, flamboyant ways as well.

'That's all very well,' we can hear you saying, 'but what happens when my mother expects me to organise her 50th wedding anniversary and I don't want to, but feel obliged? What happens when my colleague at work pouts all day and won't talk to me when we need to make joint decisions? What happens when my lover makes me feel guilty when I want an evening out with my friends? What am I supposed to do then? Fling myself on the floor and cry or storm about banging my fists on the table?'

In these two status games we've had you play with raising and lowering your status quite dramatically, just for the fun of it. We've had you go to the extremes of status behaviour so that you can see what's possible. Although it might be fun to imagine charging about throwing your weight around as a high-status person or weeping in a heap at someone's feet, those behaviours are not exactly practical on a day-to-day basis.

However, there are some very practical and very positive aspects of high and low status that will come in useful to you in real-life situations, particularly when you find yourself being manipulated against your will.

Mind the gap

When you are being manipulated, hanging on to your present status seems the right thing to do. It isn't. It will make you even more vulnerable to manipulation. That is why we have had you look at extremes in status.

These extremes are not necessarily what you *would* do, but what you *could* do. By being silly about it all, you also get a chance to inject some humour into what was originally a difficult situation for you.

Now we're going to look at just how you can use some of this behaviour without going quite so over the top. The following lists include the sort of behaviours we associate with high and low status, some of which can be assumed with very little effort.

Playing a 'ten': positive aspects of high-status behaviour

- Be physically higher than the other person.
- Take your time.
- Use silence.
- Stand tall, shoulders back.
- Speak in a very deliberate, firm voice.
- Repeat yourself.
- Listen without comment.
- Be above the argument.
- Stand your ground.
- Maintain very strong eye-contact.
- Avoid getting side-tracked by superfluous arguments.
- Make no excuses, offer no explanations.
- Have very clear boundaries.

Playing a 'one': positive aspects of low-status behaviour

- Physically get on the same level or below the other person.
- Speak in a low, sympathetic voice.
- Exhibit lots of empathy and understanding.
- Acknowledge the other person's feelings.
- Be sad or disappointed on their behalf.
- Look down.
- Use sympathetic body posture.
- Overdo apology and niceness.
- Also have very clear boundaries.

Now let's look at how to put these behaviours into effect.

People who are particularly good at wrong-footing, flustering or otherwise putting you at a disadvantage, create a tension between you and them. It may be deliberate, but in many cases it isn't.

What is created between you is what we call a status gap.

Any time there is a large gap between two types of behaviour, there is going to be tension. For instance, during a confrontation over working late: if someone starts bullying and intimidating you and you stand there and take it without a fight, that person raises their status while you're staying the same.

If they bust into tears, becoming very low status, and say you don't really care about them, and you maintain your status and stand there feeling helpless and at sea, the status gap between you is very wide. You've suddenly been made a bad, uncaring person while they are obviously suffering.

In the first instance, you're frightened into giving in; in the second you feel sorry for the other person and guilty for wanting to disagree and end up capitulating. In both cases there is a wide gap in the way you are behaving with each other, and it's in that gap you get caught off guard, become unsure and lose your way. You've done nothing but hold onto the status quo and yet you lose and then you get manipulated.

When someone wants you to knuckle under, they will widen the status gap. It's a very effective way to get you to alter your behaviour to suit their needs. All the while that there is that tension, you get drawn into the other person's agenda of what they want the outcome to be. You don't stand a chance – at least, not yet you don't.

You do, however have the ability to close the gap and even put yourself in the driver's seat by deliberately raising or lowering your own status to your advantage. This doesn't require that you fight them.

So how do you close the gap?

Using the model of one to ten to denote the full range of status available to you, you can think of status tension as any time the numbers are more than four digits away from where they should be (eg if the boss is a 'nine' and the employee is a 'five' that's a status gap; if the boss is a 'nine' and the employee is a 'three', that's six digits out of kilter and the status gap is too great).

Status tension can be created by reversing the 'normal' status quo, for instance, if the boss acts like a 'five' and the employee acts like a 'seven'. It appears as though the status gap is only two, and therefore all is well. All is not well, however, if the boss has dropped *below* the employee and is being manipulated. Therefore, for our purposes, the status gap is six digits out of kilter and needs adjusting.

We're going to show you two examples, using the high and the low ends of the status spectrum, to illustrate how to close the status tension gap.

Raising your status

Hassid's story:
Hassid is a middle manager for a car-hire firm. He's quite a gentle soul, he likes harmony around him and for everyone to get on.

Unfortunately for him, he has a secretary who likes to get her own way and is quite willing to do whatever she needs to do to get it. She is definitely not nice, is always mouthing off about how hard she works and how she never even has time for a coffee break.

Hassid knows this isn't completely true. Yes, there are periods when things do get very busy, particularly at holiday time, but Audrey wasn't that overworked.

Of course she wasn't, because Hassid was afraid to give her all the work that she was supposed to do! If he brought her more than one job at a time, she snapped at him and told him how busy she was. If he asked her to send a fax or photocopy a batch of rental agreements, she told him to do them himself, she didn't have the time. Besides, she didn't like doing routine tasks; she wanted to do more interesting things and less mindless work.

Quite simply, Hassid was afraid of his own secretary. What's more, he was afraid to tell any one else he was afraid because he thought they'd think him ineffectual and weak. So he suffered in silence, doing all the boring jobs his secretary didn't want to do which usually meant working through part of his lunch-hour and occasionally staying late.

She was acting out a 'ten' while he was playing a 'four' or a 'five'; not exactly the best ratio for a boss/secretary relationship. Hassid had to learn how to close the gap by raising his status to just above hers without becoming a tyrant, something he could never be anyway.

He had to find a way to make that shift in status without losing the soft-spoken manner which he liked in himself. Not as difficult as it may sound. He learned how to exaggerate the very qualities that got him into trouble in the first place, while maintaining a very high-status demeanour.

In their previous encounters, Hassid would back off as soon as Audrey snapped at him and retreat to his office. Once he'd done one of our workshops, he knew he had to change the status quo without necessarily radically changing his normal behaviour.

The next time Audrey had a go at him he simply waited. He didn't say anything, but he didn't retreat back into his office. He stood there patiently and quietly, two very high-status moves: silence unnerves people, especially if they are very talkative. She continued to tell him how busy she was and he continued to stand in silence.

When she finally ran out of steam, he put the papers on her desk, and said, 'In your own time, then' and only then did he return to his office. He didn't wait for an assent from her, nor did he give her any time to come back with a retort. He bided his time by acting just that little bit more in control of the situation than she was – just a notch or two above her bossy behaviour.

But he didn't have to boss back. He could be high status and still maintain the part of his personality he liked without having to raise his voice, demand she listen to him or try to bully her into submission, which would so patently not work.

Lowering your status

Exactly the same can be done at the opposite end of the status spectrum – the low end. Simon's story is a good example of how to use low status to keep yourself from getting manipulated.

> Simon is very confident and forceful in the workplace and tends to live his work life as a 'ten' or even above. He's considered rather hard-nosed. He is a TV presenter and strikes a hard bargain when renegotiating his contracts and getting the deals he wants. He's clear, he tells people

what he thinks and he usually gets what he wants.

Which is a good thing, because he ends up supporting every lover he lets into his life. As soon as he enters a personal relationship, he somehow loses his confidence and gets manipulated and taken advantage of.

He is continually attracted to partners who don't work or are in debt, who move in when he doesn't really want them to and in general, make things very difficult for him: he's usually bailing someone out of some trouble or other. He gives the kind of loans that don't get paid back. Simon gets 'suckered' into doing things for other people he doesn't really want to do because they appeal manipulatively to his better nature.

Simon's latest relationship started out the same way: he feels guilty because he was doing so well and his lover was a 'struggling artist' on the dole. Greg tried every trick in the book: when he and Simon would go out for a walk, he'd stand looking in the windows of art supply shops, sighing deeply because he couldn't afford the sable brushes that would be perfect for his latest work. He shrugged helplessly when they did the grocery shopping, saying he just didn't know where his dole money had gone.

When Simon suggested he might think about getting a part-time job and that with his connections he could find him a not too taxing one, Greg was ready with a catalogue of excuses about why he needed to have his days free: because of the light, because he works best in the day, because he needs to be able to go to museums and galleries to look at other artists' work.

When Simon suggested a part-time evening job, Greg had another catalogue of excuses: that would mean they'd never see each other, he'd be too tired to paint the next day; and what about their sex life. He usually ended these occasional discussions with the *coup de grace* that Simon didn't like his paintings and didn't want him to succeed. Simon usually replied quite heatedly that of course he cared, how could Greg think he didn't care and then was well and truly hooked into Greg's agenda.

Simon never needed too much of this before he caved in completely. The sable brushes were bought, the groceries were taken care of without comment and he stopped mentioning part-time jobs.

Greg used low-status manipulation to get his way. He lowered his status so that the gap between his despair and Simon's attempts at getting his life back seemed very wide – too wide to bridge without Simon coming across as unfeeling. Greg's status was a 'one' or 'two' while Simon's reasonableness came across as an 'eight' or 'nine'. Of course, inside Simon was feeling used and out-manoeuvred.

When Simon did our course, he became aware that *he* could use low status as a way to narrow the status gap. What he learned was that he didn't need to lower himself *below* Greg's status but just keep a couple of numbers above him to lessen the tension.

Simon learned that when Greg started to put the pressure on by sighing, 'Things are so difficult for young artists,' he could show enormous sympathy and understanding by saying, 'I know, it must be very hard; you've certainly chosen a tough career, you've got a lot of guts.' When Greg said, 'You can't possibly know what it's like,' Simon could agree and say, 'No, of course I don't know what it's like, I'm not you, but I'm really happy to hear whatever you have to say about it so I can understand better.'

In other words, he could lay on the sympathy without having to lay out the cash. When Greg looked longingly at sable brushes, Simon could agree how good they'd be to have and wonder how long it would take Greg to save up for them.

If Greg tried his usual coup de grace of 'you don't really care', Simon could now say, 'I'm so sorry you feel that way, I had no intention of giving that impression – I can't really help you out this time but I certainly do care.' By altering his status to just slightly above Greg's he didn't have to get hooked into having no-win arguments that wore him down.

What he was doing in this version of the relationship was to narrow the gap, lessen the tension and most importantly, not get drawn into Greg's agenda which is all about getting Simon to give him what he wants.

Simon's story illustrates how by choosing to change your status you can alter the outcome of your usual discussion loops and be more in charge of your side of the transaction, instead of holding on grimly to your end of the status quo, whilst being manipulated against your will.

Low-status manipulation is a real and effective way to stay nice and still manage the situation to your benefit for a change.

Low status and being too nice

One of the things that we particularly like about using low status to alter the status quo is that you are able to use a lot of your regular nice behaviour by choice and for a specific effect. Instead of having your sympathy used as a way to hook you into doing something you don't want to do, you can now use your sympathy and caring responses while at the same time not engaging with the problem or taking it on as your own.

Here's another example.

> Let's say you have a daughter and one day she corners you, acting like a number 'two' by whining and pleading with you to let her go away for the weekend and please, please, please could you pay for her share. You start defending your status as the parent by acting like an 'eight' – being firm and telling her all the rational reasons why you can't afford it and why she has to stay around for the weekend to get all her chores done. If you stick with this attempt to manage the situation, you're in deep trouble.
>
> Either she'll step up the pressure and lower her status even more, creating more of a gap till you give in; or you'll suddenly widen the gap yourself by becoming a tyrant and telling her she'd better do what she's told or else. If you give in, you'll feel you've lost another contest you didn't want to be in, in the first place. If you become the stern parent you'll feel like an ogre for having to bully her into compliance.

A gap-narrowing solution is to lower yourself to just above her pleading with lots of 'I know, I know, I can really see how much you want to go. I really wish we could help out. Isn't it terrible that we're all strapped for cash right now. What a shame you're going to have to miss out. It's so disappointing for you.' Heap on the sympathy and concern without the logical reasons why she can't go; give her lots of acknowledgement of her disappointment without turning yourself into someone she can internally accuse of being a meanie.

By over-using your niceness you can avoid getting manipulated. You can even overwhelm people with your apologies while still not giving in. 'I'm sorry, I'm so, so sorry I can't help you out this time. What must you think of me. I'm always so available, but it's such a shame I can't do it this time. I'm really, really sorry. Will you ever forgive me? Isn't this just terrible?' and so on.

Believe us, if you do this a couple of times with people who are used to getting you to do things their way, *they will stop*.

Another way to look at changing your status is by treating the other person as a different status. In other words, if you want to raise your status, think of ways of lowering the other person's. If they are acting as a 'ten' and you can't quite figure out how to become a 'fifteen', treat them as though they were a 'five'. That immediately raises you and lowers them.

Playing the numbers game: changing your behaviour on a whim

We've spent the last few pages looking at the two ends of the status spectrum and giving you some hints on how to close the status gap. We've included some of the very positive ways you can use changes in status to change what happens to you in difficult situations.

Now you're ready to play the numbers game, rather than try to figure out the best way to behave. You don't have to work out the 'right' way; you don't have to work out all the angles; you don't have to analyse the potential consequences. That's what the old you would do and you'd be back where you've always been – swimming around in the feelings and sinking fast.

It is only when you start imagining dire consequences that you believe your choice is limited.

What if, instead of getting bogged down in 'What should I do next?', you simply decided to play a 'ten'? Without any deep thought whatsoever you just acted 'ten-like'?

Or, what if you decided to act one-like, instead of trying to figure out how to win?

You already know how to behave like a 'ten'. You don't have to think about it very much. Imagine right now being a 'ten': how would a 'ten' be sitting, how would a 'ten' be looking out at the world, how would a 'ten' expect to be treated? Do the same, thinking about being a 'one': how would a 'one' be sitting right now, how would a 'one' be seeing the world or expect to be treated? Using numbers to change your behaviour instead of pre-planning and then worrying about the outcome is playing a game.

If the next time you wanted to ask for a raise you decided to play the numbers game, think about what you'd do. A 'ten' would be direct and clear, sitting tall, looking the boss in the eye, having a calm demeanour. A 'ten' would not justify, a 'ten' would lay the facts out and wait, using silence to make a point. A 'ten' would not be put off by excuses of company redundancies and cutbacks but would simply repeat the request and wait again.

If the next time you found yourself being pushed into doing something you definitely didn't want to do (such as the school-run for the umpteenth time) and you decided to play the numbers game, think about what you'd do then. A 'one' would be over-apologetic. A 'one' would be oozing sympathy for the other person's plight but be ever so sorry that they couldn't help out. A 'one' would be practically wailing on the other person's behalf, all the while being very clear they couldn't possibly help out.

You don't have to think about your behaviour when you play the numbers game. We know people who now carry around a ten of hearts from a deck of cards in their wallets to remind them that they have a 'ten' inside them when they need it. One person we know even framed a 'ten' for his office desk.

If the idea of plunging in at the deep end and dealing with the next difficult situation in this way causes you a frisson of disquiet, here are a few situations to practise on which have absolutely no consequences that could trip you up.

- The next time you go to a pub, go up to the bar, act like a 'one' and see how long it takes to get served. The longer it takes, the more successful you are.

- Then the next time you go up to the bar, act like a 'ten'. The least amount of time it takes to get served is your win this time.
- Walk down your local high street as a 'ten' and see if anyone gets in your way. If you can cut a swathe down the middle of the pavement, you've got your win.
- Walk down your high street as a 'one', getting out of people's way, even stepping into the gutter to avoid putting anyone out.
- Stand at a zebra crossing as a woebegone 'one' and watch the cars whizz by (or not since as a low status person, your eyes are downcast anyway). Again, your win is when you have to wait an inordinate length of time.
- Try striding out into the zebra crossing as a 'ten'. Be careful with this one, since we don't want you to get run over by selfish drivers many of whom no longer seem to stop at zebra crossings! Make sure you look those drivers in the eye.

These are elementary ways to practise changing your behaviour at will, on a whim and with no consequences to worry about. They may seem simple, but they will add to your collection of small wins along with your new answering machine message and apologising for apologising.

And the great fun of playing the numbers game is that no one knows you're doing it but you. Gradually, as you collect your wins, a new you will be emerging.

Status reversal

There are some situations where using a number to change your behaviour at will isn't so clear-cut, even though status manipulation is what's going on.

Dealing with your parents may be one of those situations for you. One of the trickiest areas where we find ourselves being low status from a negative point of view is when we are with our parents. This may not be true for everyone, but many people, even though they are now adults, still feel and behave like a toddler or adolescent in the presence of their parents. They become infantile, they become cowed and frightened, they become short-tempered and irritable.

The more their parents treat them like a four- or ten- or fifteen-year-old, the more they behave in that way, and so the cycle goes around and around.

Many parents and children get caught up in the difficulty of letting go of their old relationship and developing a new one. There have been many books written about the dynamics between children and parents and the issues of separation. It is not our intention to deal with the psychology of this very charged relationship.

However, what we can look at here are some of the things that you can do to loosen the grip that one or both of your parents have on you, without tearing apart the entire relationship.

If you revert to an adolescent when you are with your parents, you become powerless to break patterns of behaviour that have been established over many years. You've been practising these well-rehearsed routines most of your life. They are dispiriting in their familiarity, but also comfortably uncomfortable in their regularity.

These well-worn interchanges are like verbal ping-pong. The ball gets hit back and forth and back and forth. Every once in a while one of you scores a point and claims victory; but the next time you meet, you're both there with paddles in hand, back and forth and back and forth.

In your fantasy life you may imagine:

1. Your parents suddenly becoming understanding, tolerant and supportive of the person you have become.
2. Yourself snapping at them and telling them to stop treating you like a baby.
3. Creating a huge scene telling them how horrible and unsupportive they've been to you and how you can't stand them and never want to see them again.

Some of you may even have put '2' or '3' into effect; it's certainly been known to happen. But most of you will simply have kept the extreme forms of action well hidden in your fantasies.

If you are someone who adopts a low-status posture in the face of your parents' high-status behaviour, then you can see that this makes for a large status tension gap. Trying to act like a 'ten' or a 'one' in the face of this gap may not be as successful as in other situations – especially since there's so much history to get in the way.

One of the things that works very well in many difficult parent–child relationships is what we call status reversal. It may not work with all parents. You are the only one who can judge whether it might work with yours, but we recommend you give it a try.

It literally means that you become parent-like in a form of role reversal. Now, we don't mean becoming the critical, judgemental, impatient parent that many of you will be familiar with, but the understanding, sympathetic, nurturing parent that tends to exist in fantasy and story books and occasionally in real life.

We do not mean being patronising or treating your parents as though they were imbeciles either. Nor do we mean the kind of role reversal where you end up taking care of your parents because they suddenly become helpless in your presence.

When your parents become upset with something you've done, treat them as though they were a one-year old who needed infinite patience and understanding. We'll use Renée's story as an example.

She is in her late 20s and moved to Glasgow from Paris three years ago to be with her British boyfriend. That was certainly the first thing that upset her parents. Many more were to follow, including postponing her further education.

Renée was already intimidated by her father, which was probably part of the reason she fell in love and went to live with a man who put a bit of distance between her and him. She did return 'home' (with dread) for holidays and endured his criticism and cross-examination ('When are you going to come to your senses and come home?' 'When are you going to go back to University?' etc).

It was particularly gruesome at mealtimes when the atmosphere would get very charged and one of two things would happen. Either Renée would withdraw, stay silent and sulk into her plate, or she'd have an argument with her dad to try to deal with feeling small and insignificant in his presence. Her mother tried to keep the peace but with the two of them that always proved futile.

With either tactic the status tension gap was just too great for them to get even remotely close to talking calmly with each other. Their adversarial form of communication had become such a well entrenched habit that it was going to take something radically different to break this particular stalemate.

We worked with Renée on status reversal, where she took on the understanding parental role and treated her father as a child who needed calm reassurance and a firm hand. One of the first changes in becoming parental was for her to take the initiative, instead of waiting for the inevitable list of questions.

The next time Renée went home (Christmas, which is often fraught at the best of times) she decided to put the new tactic into practice and this was how the status reversal played itself out.

Renée: 'Dad, you haven't told me what's been happening at work lately. Did you end up making those three people redundant?'

Father: 'Yes, as a matter of fact, I was forced to do that, and right before Christmas. Made me feel awful. But what about you? I hope you're planning on spending longer than your usual three days.'

Renée: 'That's really terrible you had to do that. I hope they know it wasn't your fault and that you fought to keep their jobs. I know you'd love me to stay longer; it's always disappointing for both of you when I dash in and out for just a few days.'

Father: 'Well, you could do something about it if you really wanted to. I don't understand why you have to be in Scotland anyway. You have everything you want right here and then you could meet a nice French boy.'

Renée: 'I could, couldn't I? You must really miss me to want me to come back. That would be a giggle: we'd probably end up killing each other. Now, come on, Dad, tell me about work.'

Father: 'You keep changing the subject, I want to talk about your education that you've so cavalierly thrown away.'

Renée: 'I know you want to talk about me. And right now, I'd like to talk about you for a change. Let's talk about me another time.'

In Renée's case that was all that was needed to break the loop. For others it may take longer and may take three or four tries before you yourself get the hang of being gently parental.

Janice's story is different and demonstrates another way of using role or status reversal to change the dynamic between parent and child. Janice is typical of people who are strong and capable in all the areas of their lives, except when you put them in a room with one or both of their parents. Then this compliant, adaptive, frightened child appears from nowhere.

Janice is an advertising executive, has a strong marriage, and from the outside, has a life that looks well managed. And it is, until Mum comes along. She rings Janice at least three times every day, at work or at home, and Janice never tells her it's not a good time to talk or that even one call a day would be better.

She takes her mother shopping every week even though she doesn't want to and generally chauffeurs her around despite the fact that her mother has her own car. Janice is seething inside but is petrified to mention even the smallest inconvenience to her mother.

It would be naive to imagine that dealing with parents is the same as dealing with the rest of the world. It was important for Janice to understand that this one wasn't going to be 'handled' in one go. She had to slow things down and make it easier for herself.

First she had to notice just how impatient she got when her mother demanded things of her. So to start with, rather than show that impatience in an underhand way Janice began to treat her mother in a comforting parental way, telling her how she understood how lonely she was and how she wished she (Janice) was around more.

Then she talked to her mother about her work just the way an adult would to an older child, explaining what she did and inviting her mother to understand the huge responsibilities she had to deal with every day.

When she practised these approaches enough times she noticed that her mother didn't ring her at work as much. She never actually had to tell her mother not to ring her, but by being included in what Janice's work life was like, her mother realised that phoning so often probably wasn't a very good idea.

By then Janice was feeling better about mentioning the shopping, letting her mother know she liked spending time with her but found the regular shopping trips difficult. But most important she just felt better about being with her mother because it had become less an obligation and more a choice.

Here are some 'dos and don'ts' that we suggested to Renée and Janice and to many others who presented parents as their main difficulty. These reminders are very useful when attempting status reversal:

- Avoid making the other person feel they are wrong or try to convince them that you're right.
- Be as patient as is humanly possible.
- Listen to what the other person is saying and acknowledge their feelings.
- Avoid getting drawn into childish arguments (such as coming home and meeting a nice French boy).
- Avoid explaining the unexplainable (such as why you're going to stay in Glasgow with your boyfriend).
- Avoid accusing the other person of trying to control your life, which is probably what it feels like.
- Avoid verbal ping-pong.
- Keep returning to things that you want to talk about.

Although we have developed the idea of status reversal specifically in relation to parents, it's a useful tactic in many other situations as well. Any time that you feel someone is being heavily parental (in the negative sense), you might consider changing your own status and making them the child.

The Status Game is play: you can choose to play one day and choose not to play the next. You can choose to play it high or choose to play it low.

Whatever you choose, playing the status game is yet another way to refine your ever-expanding art of saying no.

8

I NEVER WIN:
MAKING CONFLICT WORK FOR YOU

Anything to keep the peace

Nice people don't like conflict. When you turned the page and saw the heading for this chapter, did your heart sink? When we get to this point on our workshops, a groan usually echoes around the room: couldn't we just skip this part?

How do you deal with conflict? Do you relish having the odd verbal dust-up or do you find ingenious ways to avoid ever disagreeing? Are you someone who's a smoother-over of other people's upset while swallowing your own? Are you someone who sidesteps confrontation before you get caught up in it?

Unless you are an unusual nice person, you probably don't like quarrelling, arguments and bickering at all. Since disharmony around you may reflect the disharmony you feel inside yourself, you will have devised very clever ways of pretending the conflict that's around you isn't happening.

You might acquire temporary deafness and just not hear what other people are saying. You may have developed skilful ways of detaching yourself from the proceedings: you might have an urgent meeting to go to or a train to catch or work to catch up on as you sidle out of the battle ground.

You may act like Switzerland: neutral in the face of conflict happening all around you. You may be someone who always sees both sides of the argument so you never have to take sides. Or be someone who agrees to disagree so that nothing ever gets dealt with openly.

You may make light of difficult or tense situations so that you don't have to confront the seriousness of a problem. This way you keep things on a very surface level just in case what's down a layer or two is unpleasant.

You may make yourself so invisible and self-effacing that you can vanish when it looks as though there's trouble brewing. Or you can go into the previously mentioned trance state and stay oblivious to potential danger. You may prevaricate, telling the odd white lie, stalling in order to postpone the moment of truth which later lands you deep in an argument you don't want to be in.

You may dislike conflict so much that you simply give in as soon as you get a whiff of it in the air. You may put up token resistance, but in the end you know you're going to make things all right for other people, give them what they want, let them have their own way, let them believe they're right and you're wrong.

You'll agree when you disagree. You'll make other people's absurd arguments acceptable by defending the indefensible. You'll justify someone else's bad behaviour so that you don't have to admit how upset or hurt you are and thus possibly trigger a row. You may even end up apologising when someone else is upset even though it has absolutely nothing to do with you.

If you are someone who avoids conflict, a sample disagreement might sound something like the one outlined below:

> The Other Person (TOP) could be your partner, a colleague, a friend, a relative; it doesn't matter. For the purposes of this exercise pick someone with whom you have difficulty and imagine having this conversation with them.
>
> TOP: 'Could you do me a favour?'
>
> You: 'Well, it depends on what it is.'
>
> TOP: 'I need you to drive across town to pick up something that's just come in from Herbert's.'

You: 'Well, I'm not sure. I'm sort of busy most of the day.'

TOP: 'What's one more trip then? Listen, someone's got to do it and I'm stuck here all day.'

You: 'Yes, but it's really not very convenient; it's a bit out of my way. I'm just not sure I can fit it in.'

TOP: 'Come on, it's not that far out of your way. You're always so good at fitting things in. You know I rely on you.'

You: 'Yes, but I do have a few other things I've got planned. Nothing that couldn't be moved, I suppose.'

TOP: 'Well, there you are then – whatever else you've got planned can't be all that important. And this is really important.'

You: 'Hmm, I just don't know, I'm not really sure.'

TOP: 'Now, come on. We really don't want to stand here all day arguing. Time's getting on. You're not going to disappoint me, are you?'

You: 'Well, I guess...'

TOP: 'Good; I knew I could count on you. Here's the address. See you later.'

Do you see any of yourself in this example? Is your language of adaptation like that in the conversation above? In this example you don't come right out and say 'no'. You use lots of 'not sures' and 'yes, buts', and of course, in the end (which didn't take all that long to get to) you capitulate. The other person knows just how to play on your vanity and your guilt to keep you in line.

In other words, you're a pushover and once again you get manoeuvred into doing something you don't want to do.

Every once in a while you might build up enough of a storehouse of anger and resentment to flip over unexpectedly to the nasty end of the spectrum. When you've had just about enough from the world you blow: sometimes at the right target, often at the inappropriate one. Then the conflict might look something like this:

TOP: 'Could you do me a favour?'

You: 'Well, it depends on what it is.'

TOP: 'I need you to drive across town to pick up something that's just come in from Herbert's.'

You: 'Well, I'm not sure. I'm sort of busy most of the day.'

TOP: 'What's one more trip then? Listen, someone's got to do it and I'm stuck here all day.'

You: 'Why do I always have to be the one to do your fetching and carrying? I'm fed up with always being at everyone's beck and call. Don't you ever think of getting off your own backside and taking care of these things yourself? Oh no. Why bother when you've always got old muggins here to do it instead.'

TOP: 'What's got into you all of a sudden? I just asked for a simple favour.'

You: 'Nothing's got into me all of a sudden. And it's never a simple favour with you, is it? You're so inconsiderate; you never think of anyone but yourself. Why don't *you* pick it up for a change.'

TOP: 'Touchy, touchy. All right, be difficult. That's the last time I'll ask you for a favour then.'

You: 'That'll be the day.'

Any of that sound familiar? You may have let off some steam, but what did it actually get you? In this version you used lots of accusation and blame. The conflict didn't even have a chance to progress in stages: it escalated from nought to sixty in two seconds.

Or maybe you actually do enter the fray but get caught up in the verbal ping-pong we mentioned in the last chapter which might be something like this:

TOP: 'Could you do me a favour?'

You: 'Well, it depends on what it is.'

TOP: 'I need you to drive across town to pick up something that's just come in from Herbert's.'

You: 'Well, I'm not sure. I'm sort of busy most of the day.'

TOP: 'What's one more trip then? Listen, someone's got to do it and I'm stuck here all day.'

You: 'You're always asking me to go out of my way when you know how busy I am.'

TOP: 'How am I supposed to know how busy you are? If you don't want to do me this favour, then just say so.'

You: 'I didn't say I wouldn't do it; I'd just like some consideration once in a while.'

TOP: 'Oh, boy, here we go again.'

You: 'What do you mean, here we go again? All I said was...'

TOP: 'I know what you said. You said I'm inconsiderate and I never think of you.'

You: 'I never said that. You're misinterpreting what I said. You always do that – you just hear what you want to hear.'

TOP: 'What are you accusing me of now?'

You: 'I'm not accusing you of anything. Stop being so paranoid.'

TOP: 'Yes you are. You just did; you said I was paranoid.'

And so on. The something that has to be picked up at Herbert's has been forgotten.

Here the two of you take all the old arguments out of mothballs to hurl at each other. Each of you is stuck in your well-entrenched self-righteousness so that whatever the conflict was in the first place gets lost in the slanging match. Did any of that seem familiar?

In version one you tap-danced around the issue so that you never clearly said what you wanted. In version two you went straight for the jugular and you know that at some point you'll have to go back and apologise. In version three you just perpetuated the appalling communication treadmill that goes round and round without getting anywhere.

In all three versions you end up floundering because the conflict is unpleasant and goes nowhere. All you are certain of is that you will feel bad and you will reconfirm how hopeless you are at conflict anyway.

And indeed, nice people are, in the main, hopeless at it. From all our work over the years dealing with the way people communicate, we've found that there are three main reasons why nice people find conflict so difficult.

The first is that, from the outset, you've already assumed you're going to lose. Most nice people see themselves as relatively weak when it comes to holding their own in a fight so whenever they enter into a conflict they take with them a sense of 'What's the point. I know I'll give in in the end anyway.' That hidden agenda is a dead giveaway and quickly becomes a self-fulfilling prophecy. If you believe you're going to lose, then in most cases you will.

The second is our old favourite, fear of consequences. If you enter into conflict you enter into the unknown. You don't know what may happen (unless, of course you've entered the conflict lugging your communication treadmill with you, and then you know exactly what you're going to get). You may trigger someone's rage, they might burst into tears, they might throw something at you or worse, physically abuse you. You don't know, and that not knowing will get your brain making up all sorts of things that may or may not happen.

The third reason why conflict can be so difficult is that your old family conflicts will resonate within you. If you hated seeing and hearing your parents or other adults argue and felt helpless to stop what is a very frightening experience for a child, then that feeling of helplessness will come back when, as an adult, you find yourself on the brink of a conflict. You will re-experience those old feelings and may find it hard to distinguish between what you felt then and what you are feeling now.

You may have other reasons for sidestepping disagreements which are important for you to identify, but in general, these three will be pivotal in ensuring that you avoid conflict.

Why have it?

What is conflict for? There must be a reason why it exists. Here are a few that participants in our workshops have suggested:

- To win.
- To let the other person know your opinion.
- To get your own way.
- To not get pushed around.
- To let the other person know they're wrong.
- To mark out your territory.
- To gain power over a situation.

Some of those may be the reasons why we *think* we enter into conflict; none of them are the reasons for it. Whether it is global or personal, there is only one reason for having conflict.

The purpose of conflict is to arrive at a resolution.

However, whether it is global or personal, most people do not enter conflict in order to arrive at a resolution: they do it because they want to be right. And in order for you to be right, someone else has to be wrong.

Whether it's because you want the land that I have; or you think your god is better than my god; or because you want power over me; or because you think your political system will work better than mine; or because you want me to help you with the washing up – most conflict will be about winning and losing, about getting your way over someone else's way.

Entering into conflict using one of the above reasons for doing so will not create resolution. Bludgeoning someone into submission might end the conflict – it won't resolve it. If you give in and comply with someone else's wishes, the conflict is over. If you lose your temper and later have to apologise and admit you were wrong, the conflict is over. If you argue as you huff and puff on your treadmill, well, then the conflict is never over; things may go quiet for a while, but it will be there ready to flare up again.

In none of these situations is the conflict resolved.

The parties involved in the hot spots of the world where conflict seems to continue uncontrollably year after year aren't interested in resolution. They're interested in winning.

The people on both sides of a family feud that's been going on for decades, involving each new generation in the fight, aren't interested in resolution. They're interested in being right. The original slight that caused the feud is no longer the point.

The couple who bicker at the slightest provocation, having the same argument they've been having ever since they got together, aren't interested in resolution. They're interested in fighting for the autonomy they think they lost when they became a couple. So they battle to score points in order to shore up their side.

When your pride has been injured, your feelings hurt, your dignity infringed, your sensitivities trampled over, your intelligence questioned, your abilities scorned, your passions criticised, you will want to strike out and strike back.

If, however, you never enter into conflict, there can be no resolution: either of your feelings or of the situation that caused you to be upset in the first place. If you're too nice, you will swallow the impulse to strike out and strike back and carry on as though nothing untoward has happened. It has of course, but for you, it might simply be too frightening to do anything but endure the feelings, which of course then get added to the storehouse of all the other hurts, injuries and criticisms you've endured before.

When you do, on occasion, enter into conflict, you carry a whole history of losing and submitting along with you. This often means that even though you may be arguing about one issue, all the other issues that have remained unresolved begin to fight for a chance to be heard.

Then winning does become incredibly important. It's almost as though once you've actually worked up the courage to speak your mind, you *have* to win in order to prove an ancient and very sore point. It's very hard for some people to give up wanting to win, at almost any cost, once they've launched themselves into the hostilities.

So given all this, is resolution ever possible in the face of being too nice? If you either run away from the combat zone entirely or enter it with trepidation, ready to hold up the white flag of surrender at a moment's notice, or go in with your sword already drawn, can you ever get to a place of resolution?

Conflict resolution

To resolve a problem is to find a solution to it. All right, if the purpose of conflict is to arrive at a resolution, why isn't me getting my way a resolution? Why isn't letting the other person know they were wrong a resolution? Why isn't demanding my rights a resolution? Why isn't getting an apology a resolution?

All of those may seem a form of resolution, but if you leave the other person feeling as bad as you felt before, then you haven't solved the problem. It's still about winning. Letting the other person know the distress you feel may be part of the solution, but if that's what your true purpose is, then you won't get very far.

On our workshop we use the idea of resolving conflict on a win-win basis; a situation where nobody loses. As with everything else we have looked at in this book, it is *a* way to resolve conflict; it is not the *only way*.

Attaining conflict resolution, or creating a win-win situation, involves a number of components – for instance:

- Not blaming or accusing.
- Moving the argument forward.
- Bridge building: giving something to the other person so that they'll want to give something to you in return.
- Finding out why you can't have what you want.
- Changing yourself in order to change others.

Before we explain what we mean by each of these components, we need to emphasise that conflict resolution requires thought; it requires a great deal of careful, considered thought. Since the way you deal with conflict now is a habit – just like all your other nice behaviour – changing the way you handle conflict will involve raising your awareness of what you already do and what doesn't work.

If you either avoid or get drawn into unresolvable conflict, then you are playing out well defined patterns of behaviour – you will follow them without a thought. Just take Pavlov's dogs, for instance. If you need reminding, Pavlov experimented with dogs, who salivated every time they got fed. He rang a bell at each feeding and continued to do this until they associated the sound of the bell with feeding so that even without being fed, they salivated when the bell rang.

For you, there will be words, phrases, physical postures, silences and actions that trigger your emotional saliva glands; and before you know it, you will be enmeshed in either disgruntled compliance, sudden explosions or endless, repetitive quarrels.

On the following pages, are some of the elements that we believe contribute to achieving conflict resolution.

Not blaming or accusing

Blaming the other person when you are unhappy can often be your first line of defence. 'It's all his fault.' 'She's to blame.' When things don't go our way we're often quick to blame someone else for our misfortune. This is particularly true if you have been storing up a lifetime of resentments, upset and anger. Then it's easy to heap the blame on the person you're in conflict with, whether they have anything to do with that storehouse or not.

Thus a lot of sentences begin with 'You': 'You only think of yourself.' 'You never take my feelings into consideration.' 'You always expect me to do what you want.' This also involves the use of the words 'never' and 'always' – creating huge, sweeping statements that keep you away from what is going on at that moment.

In order not to blame or accuse you have to stay conscious of what you are feeling and how the situation is affecting you and include that in the argument, ie: use 'I' statements, not 'you' statements.

A 'you' statement in the context of conflict means that the other person is being made responsible for the problem; they are being backed into a no-win corner; they're being made wrong and put on the defensive. Here's an example: 'You never think of me.' 'Of course I think of you.' 'When?' 'Well, a lot of the time.' 'You' statements tend to point out the inadequacies of the other person. No one likes being told they're wrong.

Think about it for yourself for a moment. Can you remember the last time someone started a sentence with 'you' when you were quarrelling? The first thing we tend to do in those situations is leap to our own defence instead of getting on with the specifics of the argument.

The subject gets diverted from the problem and suddenly gets very personal. If you want your flatmate to help with the washing up, it's unlikely that 'You never help with the washing up' is going to make them spring into the kitchen. It's an invitation for 'I do my share.' 'No, you don't,' 'Yes, I do,' etc.

In a conflict, an 'I' statement shows that you're being responsible for your side of the feelings and wants. Not blaming or referring to the other person's deficiencies means your own arguments can be put forward instead of the attention being on the accusations.

Thus, rather than saying, 'You're so inconsiderate, you always make decisions without asking me' which is accusing and backs the other person into a defensive corner, you could say, 'Next time you have to make a decision like this, I'd really like it if we could discuss it ahead of time.'

This takes the charge out of the statement. You've not only been responsible for your own feelings, you've also given the other person something quite specific that you want from them. The more you take responsibility for what you are feeling and what you want, the less you'll need to find fault and complain about the other person's behaviour.

A word of caution here. Some people who have trouble giving up the idea of winning or of making the other person wrong use 'I' statements as a bit of a blind: 'I feel you never…' 'I feel you are so inconsiderate.'

Using 'I' statements is a less threatening way to let the other person know how their behaviour or what they are saying is affecting you. 'You never ask me what I want to do' is different to 'I feel boxed into a corner when you ask me to do something I don't want to do. I don't feel I can say no.'

The first version is whiny and blaming. The second version is clear and you've given the other person a lot of information about yourself which doesn't invite a knee-jerk defence.

Moving the argument forward

This concept is particularly important for those of you who get stuck on the communication treadmill. These are arguments that just go around and around and around and never get anywhere. They usually exhaust both sides. Old hurts and upsets get recycled and trotted out yet again.

These kinds of quarrels are probably the most habitual and clearly illustrates why we say that conflict resolution requires thought. Once you get started, it's almost impossible to stop the cycle. It's bound to end in tears, slammed doors, sulks or other patterns of behaviour that are all too familiar.

A stalemate isn't a resolution. To move an argument forward something different needs to happen. If we go back to the use of language, this is an ideal time to stop yourself in mid-sentence by asking yourself, out loud, what's going on. It is a bit like 'taking a time-out'. Just as in some sporting events you can call a time out to reassess strategy or take a breather, calling a time out during an argument can give the two of you a chance to see what's going on and hopefully stop the treadmill long enough to take the argument in a new, more constructive direction.

If we take a snippet from our earlier conflict it might now go something like this:

You: 'What do you mean, here we go again? All I said was…'

TOP: 'I know what you said. You said I'm inconsiderate and I never think of you.'

You: 'I think we need to stop here because we seem to be going around in circles. We seem to be upsetting each other and then getting off the subject. Let's start again and see if we can unravel what the problem is.'

In this sample you've killed two birds with one stone. You've stopped the ping-pong game flat and you've stopped accusing and have invited joint responsibility for the next stage of the discussion.

Bridge Building

This is giving the other person something so that they will want to give you something in return. When you're in the middle of the emotional turmoil of a conflict, the idea of giving the other person something might well feel like capitulation. 'Why should I give them something when they're being so horrible to me?'

Giving something to the other person does not mean conceding to them. Let's take that trip to Herbert's again. What you want in this case is not to go; you want them to leave you alone and find someone else to do it. So what else could you give to the other person other than getting in your car and driving across town? Here's a possible solution:

TOP: 'Could you do me a favour?'

You: 'Well, it depends on what it is.'

TOP: 'I need you to drive across town to pick up something that's just come in from Herbert's.'

You: 'You've asked me at such a bad time. I'm sorry I won't be able to fit it in.'

TOP: 'But I'm relying on you to take care of this for me.'

You: 'I'm really flattered you rely on me so much. You must have a huge amount on your plate at the moment.'

TOP: 'I do, I don't know where to begin, everything seems to be happening at once. And that's why I need you to help me out.'

You: 'I can see you're snowed under. It really is a shame I can't help you out with Herbert's. I just won't be able to fit in a trip across town, but tell you what, why don't we take ten minutes right now to go over everything that's piled up and see if I can't help you sort out some priorities. And then we can try to think of someone else to help out with Herbert's. Maybe we can even convince them to deliver.'

You can't necessarily know whether that will get the desired results, but firstly you've changed the course of the argument by taking the attention off yourself and back on to the other person. Second, you've made an offer of the kind of help you might be prepared to give, which is more than they had before. Between you, you might even sort out the Herbert's problem.

In this replayed scenario, the word 'no' was never mentioned, yet the manner in which the conflict was resolved all did stem from setting a boundary and being clear – truly an art!

Think of bridge building as laying out enough planks so that the other person will want to start putting out planks of their own. In this case you offered sympathy first of all. You then offered clarity – you couldn't fit it in: no weaselly umming and ahing, no accusations, no blame. And finally, you offered them some help. Not a lot; just enough to ease the current crisis.

That means you laid out three planks from your side, quite prepared to build the bridge far enough out to meet at some point. The other person now has some new options. They can refuse to lay out any planks at all and continue to try to bully or cajole you into submission, or keep the argument going for their own purposes. Or they could decide that ten minutes of your time might be a pretty good option after all and lay down a couple of planks of their own by accepting your offer and then deciding what to do about Herbert's.

Bridge building can be quite an effective way to bring a fresh new dynamic to tired old disagreements. It can satisfy your need (or compulsive habit) to be helpful and caring without giving in; it can stop an argument from recycling itself; it can give the other person a way out of staying entrenched on their side of the argument.

Finding out why you can't have what you want

Sometimes there is no solution that can satisfy your specific want. Sometimes the circumstances just don't allow for it and you may have to accept the situation. We consider knowing that there was no other solution in the current circumstances to be a win.

Simply finding out why you can't have what you want can take the edge of not having it. However, trying to find out why you can't have what you want isn't a licence to cross-examine the other person. That just perpetuates the dynamic of accusation and blame.

By doing a small amount of probing you can take the opportunity to let the other person know how you're feeling. Finding out why you can't have what you want may also give you enough information so that you feel less resentful of the person who wouldn't give you what you wanted. Back to Herbert's again:

TOP: 'Could you do me a favour?'

You: 'Well, it depends on what it is.'

TOP: 'I need you to drive across town to pick up something that's just come in from Herbert's.'

You: 'It's not really convenient for me today. It's going to be hard for me to fit it in.'

TOP: 'I'm relying on you to help me out.'

> You: 'I really do feel taken for granted in these situations. Can't you get someone else to pick it up or have them deliver it? It would make life so much easier if I didn't have to drive all the way across town.'

> TOP: 'I'm not taking you for granted. I'm really stuck. I completely forgot about Herbert's, and now there's nothing else I can do but ask you to help me out. I'll make it up to you, I promise.'

By trying to find out why, you've given the other person the opportunity to be upfront with you. You've also let them know how you feel (without accusation) and hopefully, they really will make it up to you at some time in the future (you can even use their promise as a humorous lever yourself if they forget).

Changing what you want

Having found out why you can't have what you want, there is absolutely no reason why you can't change what you want then and there. Your want could change from not having to do what someone else wants you to do (as in the above example) to getting some acknowledgement and affirmation from the other person. And, yes, you may have to ask for it. We have heard many people say that if you have to ask for someone's praise it doesn't count. Why not?

That's one of those little rules of behaviour that says we can only value acknowledgement if it's spontaneously given. You may be someone who is adept at giving lots of praise and hands out compliments very easily. Others are not necessarily as adept and do need to be prompted. It does not mean that the applause is any less well meant.

If asking makes you feel uneasy, use some gentle humour to help it along. This is how you can change from one want to another:

> TOP: 'Could you do me a favour?'

> You: 'Well, it depends on what it is.'

TOP: 'I need you to drive across town to pick up something that's just come in from Herbert's.'

You: 'It's not really convenient for me today. It's going to be hard for me to fit it in.'

TOP: 'I'm relying on you to help me out.'

You: 'I really do feel taken for granted in these situations. Can't you get someone else to pick it up or have them deliver it? It would make life so much easier if I didn't have to drive all the way across town.'

TOP: 'I'm not taking you for granted. I'm really stuck. I completely forgot about Herbert's and now there's nothing else I can do but ask you to help me out. I'll make it up to you, I promise.'

You: 'All right, I'll do it. But I'm going to need payment in hard currency, you know.'

TOP: 'Huh? Hard currency?'

You: 'Yes. Let's see, I'll take five thank yous, ten flatterings and a promise of three favours in return. You can pay me later. Bye.'

Changing you in order to change others

All the things we have been talking about so far – 'I' statements, not 'you' statements, moving the argument forward, bridge building, finding out why you can't have what you want – require you to change, to do something different from what you have always done.

In each case, it is you who has to take the initiative to create a different communication dynamic. You've had to stop accusing, you've had to learn to call a time out and change the direction of the conflict, you've had to put down planks in order to reach out to the other person, you've had to make the effort to find out what's really going on.

You've had to move from doing what you've always done to doing something different. In other words, in order to change the other person, you have had to change yourself first. For nice people that's often very difficult to do. It would be so much easier if the other person changed first so you didn't have to.

Wanting the other person to change is one of the world's favourite 'If onlys…' There isn't a person in existence, not just nice people, who hasn't, at some point in their life, said 'If only he/she were different, then I'd be OK' or words to that effect. 'If only he'd get a job, then I'd feel more secure.' 'If only she would stop nagging, then I'd have some peace.' 'If only she'd stop sulking, then we could have a real conversation.' 'If only he'd tell me what he's feeling, then I wouldn't feel so left out' 'If only they didn't phone me so often, I wouldn't feel so guilty.'

This is you wishing that the other person would be different so that you could feel better. It keeps you in a very passive, victim-like role of waiting for the other person to change to make things all right for you. You relinquish responsibility for whatever is going on by putting the onus on them to change the outcome of the situation.

It's also a way to put your life on hold. You're sitting around waiting for your life to change, which, of course, will happen once the other person does whatever it is you want them to do to make it all all right. If you wait for the other person to change to make things all right, you'll wait for ever.

The ONLY way you can influence the outcome of a well-entrenched pattern of behaviour between you and someone else is to change your side of it. This means becoming less passive, taking responsibility for your own feelings and wants, and taking some action to create a different outcome.

The trouble here is that if you've been too nice all your life, passivity comes naturally. There is also the problem of not knowing – or at least not wanting to admit to knowing – your needs and wants. That's why it is easier for you to avoid conflict. It takes time, thought and effort to make a significant difference.

Changing yourself means paying attention to everything you say, when the potential for conflict looms large. It means catching yourself as the same well-worn words start to form in your mouth and then doing something, almost anything, different.

Changing yourself in order to change others is a potent tool for getting your choice back. It means (again, without the other person knowing) you have put yourself in charge of the direction the conflict is going to take. You are in charge of its resolution.

9

THAT'S NOT ALL THERE IS

Thus far, we've talked about some of the main techniques that make up the art of saying no; methods and tactics that we've developed for use on our workshops: language, boundary setting, status and conflict. There are many other behavioural changes that can be used in support of or in tandem with them. Some of these have been touched on briefly in other chapters and in this one we'll go into much greater detail on how they can best be used.

Getting their attention

One of the problems that you'll encounter is that having been nice for so long, some people will no longer really listen to you. They don't hear you, particularly if they don't want to hear what you have to say. They may be so used to the responses you've always given that they no longer expect anything else. This means that even if you do attempt to say something different, demand something from the other person or posit a new argument, you will be ignored.

Grabbing their attention long enough to change the course of the discussion is an important technique for the newly emerging 'not nice' person. Here are some tactics we have found especially effective for combating the defensiveness we feel when being attacked or criticised (or what you think is an attack or a criticism). You get drawn into feelings and actions that work totally against you. These techniques are very simple and require very little thought, so that if your brain does go on hold you can still fall back on these with minimal effort.

Agreement

Agreement is one of our favourite tools. It's incredibly simple to use, it has an immediate impact on the situation and it puts you absolutely in the driver's seat to change the direction of a conversation. If someone is giving you a hard time, this is a tool that you can use to stop them in their tracks.

What you want to do when someone is having a go at you is to take the wind out of their sails. You are looking to diffuse someone's bluster and to make them feel they are being a little difficult or silly.

Try agreeing with them. That's it, simply agreeing with them. If they say that you're hopeless, agree with them and say, 'You're probably right. I am hopeless.' If they say what a shambles you've made of your life, say, 'You're probably right, it is a shambles.' If they say you don't know what you're talking about, agree and say, 'You're right, I haven't a clue what I'm talking about.' Your intention here is to stop them trampling all over you and leave them with no place to go.

Normal defensive dialogue goes something like this:

TOP: 'You're hopeless.'

You: 'No, I'm not.'

TOP: 'Yes, you are. You don't get anything right. I ask you to do a simple favour and look at the mess.'

You: 'It's not a mess. I'm sure we can work something out.'

TOP: 'Yes, once I take over again.'

Agreement goes something like this:

TOP: 'You're hopeless.'

You: 'You're right. I am hopeless.'

TOP: 'I should say so, look at this mess.'

You: 'Horrible, isn't it? I never saw such a mess. I can't be trusted for a minute. Do you think there's anything on earth that can possibly be done to retrieve it all? I doubt it.'

TOP: 'What's got into you?'

You: 'I don't know. Something weird though, don't you think?'

Agreement has a startling effect on bullies.

> **Jo Ellen:** I worked for a company once that had the classic good cop/bad cop set-up or management structure which is quite common in the business environment. It can also be found in relationships and amongst parents.
>
> In this situation the chairman (who underneath was quite tough) was the good cop: he came across as a pussy cat. He loved giving people what they wanted; he loved saying yes; he loved being benevolent; he loved being the good sport. He wanted people to come to him with their problems and he would promise to sort them out.
>
> However, his managing director was the bad cop: he was the classic hatchet man. He was a bully. He took people apart; he belittled; he criticised; he mocked.
>
> While the chairman was above it all, the MD cut a swathe of destruction through the company. He did it with me ... for a while. I'd never been bullied in any of my jobs before, so I was knocked for six. I didn't know what was happening at first and after coming away shell-shocked from a couple of encounters, I decided I had to do something to save my skin from another verbal hiding.
>
> I decided to use a technique that works really well for me: agreement. Here is a synopsis of the confrontation that turned the tide. I had to prepare a report for the chairman. It had to pass by the MD first so that he could see if there was anything missing. He came down to my office,

his usual blustering self and said with no preamble, 'This report is terrible; it's a load of crap.'

Me: 'You're right. It is terrible; what a load of crap.' (He was gobsmacked for all of five seconds. Then he found his voice.)

MD: 'There are spelling mistakes.'

Me: 'Oh, I know. I'm a very creative speller. Life would be much better if you got me a spellchecker for my computer.'

MD: 'Well, you're going to have to redo this report; I can't have it going to the chairman like this.'

Me: 'You're right. It definitely needs redoing. But since I made such a hash of it the first time, and you don't think I'm very good, you probably need to get someone else to do the report who'll do a better job.'

MD: 'Oh well, it's not that bad I guess. But be sure you fix the lousy spelling.'

So ended his mini reign of terror with me. He never bothered me again (and I never did get that spellchecker). He just went and found someone else to bully who didn't know how to deal with his scare tactics.

Agreement is such a good tool for us nice people because we don't have to bully back. With bullies you need to do something to stop their aggressive behaviour (other than hitting them, we mean). Most bullies will back down if someone is aggressive back, but I, like most nice people, am not aggressive and I didn't want to have to become so in order to protect myself. Bullying back can seem quite frightening if you don't practise it on a regular basis.

A lot of advice is given that says you must stand up to a bully.

That may be very difficult if you're frightened and shaking in your boots. Agreement is a non-aggressive way to bully back. Agreement takes the wind out of someone's sails and for once they're wrong-footed instead of us. Sometimes the other person doesn't even know what you're doing; something's different, they just don't know what.

They go on the defensive for a change. Every time they criticise you, and you agree, they simply don't know where to go. They might keep coming back with, 'Well, you'd just better shape up then.' Your answer is still agreement: 'You're absolutely right. I do need to shape up.'

Agreement works.

Buying Time

Nice people respond to the demands that other people make of them. Someone will ring you up and want an answer to something right away; someone will come into your office and ask where the report is and expect you to produce it right there and then because they want it. They will ask you to marry them and expect you to say 'yes' immediately. They will invite you to dinner or a concert and expect you to say 'How wonderful, of course I'll come'.

In all these cases the other person expects to get the answer that they want and generally you give it to them, often simply because they asked you in the first place. Their assumption that you will agree wrong-foots you, as we have looked at in detail earlier in the book. It's very easy to get wrong-footed. You'll then give your habitual answer of 'Yes, the report will be ready in five minutes; Yes, I'll marry you; Yes, I'll pick up the package from Herbert's; Yes, I'll cook 16 cakes for the church fête'.

The 'no' may be in your head, but the feelings overwhelm you and the 'yes' comes out because you are in a panic. You give the response you think they want to hear, regardless of yourself. What happens is that you start operating on the other person's agenda, not your own. It's as though they set the pace of the conversation and you go along with it, even though it may be much too fast for you.

The difficulty here, is that because you are working to their agenda and not to your own, you don't yet know whether you want to go to the concert, bake the cakes or even marry the person. Your feelings of panic overwhelm you so much that you can't think straight.

Buying time allows the panic to subside just long enough to get your brain back into gear; just long enough to bring a modicum of objectivity to the situation. There are many ways to buy time and it's handy to have a few ready-made excuses to use at a moment's notice – for instance:

- 'You caught me at a really bad moment; I'll get back to you later.'
- 'I have to go to the loo; I'll be back in a sec.'
- 'There's someone at the door; I'll ring you back in a few minutes.'
- 'I can't possibly think straight till I've had my first cup of coffee. I'll get back to you after my caffeine fix.'

Jo Ellen: I saw a cartoon in *The New Yorker* that showed a man reading a newspaper looking up startled, while his wife was standing in the kitchen talking on the phone. The caption under the cartoon said, 'Sometimes a good excuse to get off the phone is hard to find' and in the bubble coming out of the woman's mouth was, 'Oh, my God, I have to go, the hyena's loose!'

Even absurd excuses are better than none. You can use anything that removes you, however briefly, from the fray. What we are looking for here is anything that gets you out of the room, off the phone, closes the door, out of the current situation, even if for only five minutes.

In the time you've bought you can pace the room, phone a friend and moan, meditate, jump up and down a few times, yell, stare at nothing, rip a phone book in half, cry, laugh, write a letter. Anything, anything to stop your normal response of compliance. Anything that breaks the other person's hold over you.

This isn't about saying no. You may not yet know whether you want to say no. You also may not know whether you want to say yes. You may indeed want to get married, finish the report, bake the cakes, etc. But if your brain is in scramble mode, you'll be agreeing to something because the other person wants it, not because you do.

You may end up giving the same response you would have given in the panic, but you won't have done it mindlessly and you won't have done it as a knee-jerk reaction to someone else's demands. You will have created a choice for yourself that you didn't have before. It may even be that, having bought time, you go away for five minutes, think about it hard, know you don't want to do it and still end up doing it, by choice. You'll have had time to weigh and measure the pay-offs and decided that even though you don't want to go to the concert, the pay-off will benefit you in the long term. You will still have created a choice for yourself.

Buying time allows you to slow down. It allows your bodily reactions time to slow down (shallow breathing, racing heart, etc). It allows time to soothe your agitation and get your thoughts together. You can then go back into the situation in a better frame of mind. We see the buying of time as a win. That's the change, not the ability to say no.

The fact that you've given yourself five minutes to go to the loo, ten minutes to drink a hot drink, even one minute to look out of the window and breathe deeply two or three times, is a win. The outcome in these situations is not relevant. It's the action that you take that changes the way you respond to it and the way you feel about it which is relevant.

Slowing the pace

There are ways of slowing the pace without breaking off entirely. You can use phrases like, 'could you just go a little slower? I'm not sure if I caught all of that.' 'I'd really appreciate if you could repeat that so I'm absolutely sure I got it all.' 'Would you explain that over again? My poor brain didn't take it all in.'

This could even be a time when you use some of those knee-jerk phrases from your adaptive language list, but this time deliberately. 'I'm so stupid, you need to go much slower so I get it all.' 'I know I'm being pathetic, but it's not making any sense to me.' Using adaptive language by choice will buy you time, slow things down and create some mental space for you to catch up.

If you're one of those people who hate to admit your confusion, you may well act as though you know what someone is saying when in truth you don't. Slowing things down on purpose will allow you to catch up on what you don't understand. You may be a gabbler, someone who gets defensive, over-explains, elaborates and otherwise carries on long after it would be wise to keep quiet. It's a great defence mechanism.

We've mentioned before that most people, nice or not, don't like silence: it makes them feel uncomfortable. Usually we leap into the silence or gaps in the conversation to stop that uncomfortable feeling.

Here's another game you can play. When you encounter a silence, see just how long it takes the other person to fill it. It's kind of like a staring contest – most people have played those at one time or another. Well this is a silence contest: I can out-wait you, just see if I can't. It may make you uncomfortable, but because you're doing it deliberately, it's the other person who's taken by surprise; you will have put them in a more difficult position.

If you practise this waiting game enough, you'll get very good at it. Silence is a very effective weapon to stop the other person from setting the usual traps that you get caught in.

If total silence just isn't possible in the circumstances, you can create your own mini gaps in the conversation by keeping your answers as short as possible. Make a statement, brief and to the point, and then keep your mouth firmly shut.

Getting your 'no' in quickly

This is a great art of saying no technique for changing what you usually do before you even think about it. As soon as a demand – any demand – is made, get your 'no' in as quickly as possible. Then, you can do all the apologising and grovelling and normal nice behaviour you want: 'I'm really, really sorry; it must sound awful me saying no; I hope you'll forgive me', etc. If you're particularly scared about saying no, throw it into the conversation immediately and then drape it over with super nice language. In an odd way this takes the charge off the 'no'.

- 'I need you to stay late to finish this draft.'
- 'No, I can't tonight. I'm so sorry, I wish I could. I really, really wish I could help you out, but it's just impossible tonight. I'm really so sorry.'

Pretty soon they'll be apologising to you for asking in the first place!

You can practise saying the word 'no' just for the sake of saying 'no', even if you know you ultimately have to do what they want. You can change your mind as soon as you've said it, be incredibly nice, apologise. But you've got the 'no' in fast and it might mean that the next time you practise the 'no', it will stay there on its own.

> TOP: 'You'll be able to do the school-run today, won't you.'

> You: 'No. Did I say no? Of course I meant yes, of course I'll do it. How silly of me.'

or

> TOP: 'I need you to stay late to finish that draft.'

> You: 'No can do. Good heavens! What did I just say? I don't know what came over me. Of course I'll stay.'

What you've done again is to change the dynamic of what usually happens in these communications. You've added something new to the equation. You've put your 'no' in first and that's what's different.

Afterwards you can do all the apologising, all the explaining, all the excuse making, all the changing of your mind, but you've got your no in up front and everyone will know it. This also makes you more burglar proof. Next time they come to ask, they'll remember your odd behaviour and think twice. It's great practice.

Wait a minute

'Wait a minute' is the shortest and easiest form of buying time we can think of. As soon as you notice something come out of your mouth that you wish hadn't, immediately say 'Wait a minute!' Or if you are aware that someone else is pushing the conversation in a direction you're not too sure about, say 'Wait a minute.'

- 'Wait a minute, did I mean to say that?'
- 'Wait a minute, I'm not sure if that's what I really think.'
- 'Wait a minute, don't hang up just yet, I have something else to say.'

- 'Wait a minute, I think before we end this meeting, everyone needs to say what's on their mind.'

Here you're just stopping the proceedings and being more in charge. You can catch yourself out. In that split second when you realise that you don't like what is happening, you can buy five seconds' worth of time by using 'Wait a minute'.

You don't know what you're going to say next. You can even say, 'Wait a minute…', not be able to think of anything, and then say, 'Oh never mind.' You've still changed the dynamic, introduced doubt, changed your pattern and had a small win.

Changing your mind

This is 'Wait a minute' after the fact. In other words, retrieving a situation at some point after it has happened. What happens when the realisation comes an hour, two days, three weeks after the fact? What do you do then?

In the same way that you may feel you have to work to someone else's agenda, you may also feel that you have no right to change your mind. 'I gave my word, I can't go back on it now.' It's as though once you've made a commitment you can't uncommit yourself. Why not?

It's as though once the situation has passed there's nothing you can do about it; it's written in stone. You said 'yes' to something and you can't change your mind. It's not allowed.

Other people change their minds all the time. Indeed you're the victim of these changes. You may have a history of people breaking their word to you and as a result tell yourself that no matter what, I'm true to my word. Good sentiments. However, they can land you in a heap of trouble.

You have the right to change your mind. Whether it's five minutes later or a month later, you have the right to say, 'That was a mistake. I'm so sorry, I'm going to have to let you down. I won't be able to…'

We've met a number of men and women on our course who actually married people because, having said 'yes', they were unable to say they had changed their minds. They knew they had made a mistake, but they got married anyway. Some people are still in those marriages; others got themselves out of them but only after years of grief.

We've met people who have changed jobs, moved cities, sold houses, given up relationships, bought the wrong car, gone on the wrong holiday, all because they felt they couldn't change their minds. In some cases it wasn't even about being scared. They truly felt that they didn't have the right to change their minds once the deal had been done.

The length of time is not the issue. Any time after a decision has been made, it can be unmade. It may mean you have to do so much apologising you may drown in the syrup, but at least you'll have got yourself out of a situation you knew was wrong for you. If this one seems impossible for you, start playing the game of changing your mind over small, inconsequential things.

Not rising to the bait

The more people are used to your behaviour, the more they know, either consciously or unconsciously, how to get you. They become practised at manipulating and manoeuvring you into doing what they want. They are good at steering conversations, disagreements and arguments in the direction they want them to go. They know how to wear you down.

One of the things that they are very adept at is dangling bait they know you will rise to. They know what words, phrases, criticisms, implications and assumptions will get you in your gut and they'll trot them out whenever you show a bit of resistance. They will throw in provocative or contentious arguments that they know you won't be able to resist.

They might tell you how you feel and what you want; they'll offer points of view and opinions that get your goat. They know you'll respond to that rather than whatever the original argument or discussion was about. They are like expert computer operators, pressing the exact buttons that will get you going off on a tangent and away from the discussion at hand. They may not realise what they're doing; it doesn't have to be deliberate – it still works. You get hooked and then they can reel you in at their leisure.

When someone does cast their line in your direction, resisting the bait will require thought on your part. It requires that you know what kind of things will get you and start you thrashing around with the hook in your mouth. You need to be alert to the dangers of the bait.

You have to resist gobbling it up and getting hooked.

It's time to be a crafty trout at the bottom of the lake that knows all the tricks in the book and swims below the lures and out of the way of the shiny hooks. 'Oh look, I've seen that bait before. You'd think they could try some fresh worms for a change. That's an old smelly one.' Try even saying it out loud to let them know you know their game.

When you don't rise to the bait and just look at it, the power dynamic changes. They will have to do something different if you aren't responding the way you always have in the past.

Not engaging

Not engaging is another form of not rising to the bait. One of the ways people try to get you hooked is to get you to explain yourself. They will demand to know what you are thinking or what the problem is. 'Why not?' is a common response when you say you can't do something that they want.

Every time you supply an excuse or offer an explanation you provide the other person with an opportunity to 'fix' the problems you present so that it works out in their favour. Here are some examples.

> You: 'So sorry, I can't help you out on this report.'
>
> TOP: 'Why not?'
>
> You: 'Well, I have to go shopping during my lunch hour because I've got some people coming to dinner tonight.'
>
> TOP: 'That's no problem. If we both work straight through lunch, then we're sure to finish before 5:30 and you can do your shopping then.'

or

> You: 'So sorry, I can't help you out with this report.'
>
> TOP: 'Why not?'

> You; 'I don't really understand the computer programme that you use for the layout all that well.'

> TOP: 'That's no problem. You do the research part and I'll deal with inputting the computer.'

If you hand them an explanation you hand them the chance to knock it right out of the way to suit their purposes. Besides, they're better at this than you are. When you set a boundary there will be some people who will weasel their way around the perimeter fence looking for the slightest weakness in your defences. Giving an excuse or an explanation is a sure signal that there is a way to get at you.

Short and sweet

As with getting your 'no' in quickly and not engaging, 'less is more' is an important axiom to keep in mind. Long-winded explanations and justifications will only get you deeper into the problem. The cliché, 'when you're in a hole, stop digging', could just as easily be re-written, 'when you're being too nice, stop talking.'

By talking too much, you give the other person enough rope to hang you with. Here's an example:

> TOP: 'I really need you to drive over to Herbert's to pick up a package.'

> You: 'I'm really sorry I can't. First I have to go shopping at Waitrose and then I promised Aunty Rose I'd stop by there. And there isn't enough petrol in the car and I'm not even sure where Herbert's is anyway.'

> TOP: 'The shopping can wait and Aunty Rose will be there tomorrow. If you leave now, you'll have time to stop at the petrol station and I'll lend you my A to Z, so you won't get lost.'

The short and sweet version:

TOP: 'I need you to drive over to Herbert's to pick up a package.'

You: 'I can't, sorry.'

TOP: 'Why not? I need you to go.'

You: 'No, I'm afraid I can't help you out.'

TOP: 'I was relying on you. What am I going to do now?'

You: 'I really can't help you out; you'll have to find someone else.'

It is another automatic reflex to want to give more information than is required. It's as though you feel obliged to give the other person lots of reasons why you can't do something they want you to do. The less information you give, the easier it will be to stand your ground when you are refusing.

Offering lots of options

When someone suggests something to you and you feel that you have to hop to it and do whatever it is the way the other person wants, try flooding the other person with lots and lots of suggestions, all the while keeping away from the one you don't want.

When you are confronted with a problem or a situation which you don't want to be in, instead of saying 'yes', come up with a list of options that shows the other person that there are many other solutions other than your doing it.

For instance, if you're always being asked to fit in extra work because you're so good at getting things done, say (in tandem with lots of regretful apology) you can't possibly do it, but supply a load of ideas that show your good intentions: you're not being difficult, you're simply not able to help out at this time and here's a list of options.

We did a workshop for a group of business people whose jobs were to be nice to people: they had to be at everyone's beck and call because of the nature of the department. It was forbidden to say 'no' to anyone.

Yet at the same time, they couldn't get all the work that needed doing done. Other people in the company were so used to calling upon this particular group that they no longer knew there was any other way to be.

We had each of these people think of the most common form of interruption they had to deal with on a daily basis and, in the quiet of the workshop space, see if they could come up with a range of possible options. What they realised was that outside the heat of the moment, they could see many other solutions to the difficulties that were not apparent when they were caught up in the immediate stress.

This is something you can do quietly, in your own time: identify the kinds of situations that make you feel there's nothing you can do but give in, then think of all the options that could be available. If possible, play this game with a friend. They won't have all the same attachments you have.

Armed with your list of options, the next time someone comes along expecting you to do what you've always done, you can take out your list and say, 'What a shame I can't help you out this time. However, I have thought of a number of ways to get around the problem so you won't miss me at all. They are …'

Giving a number of options is a different form of boundary setting. You aren't saying, this far and no farther; but you are saying, I am willing to help you out, but only insofar as I will help you identify another solution. This avoids having to say an outright 'no' and leaving the other person at a loss. Offering lots of options gets you both off the hook.

Repeating yourself

Avoid using this particular tactic too often. But, sometimes, when subtler tactics fail, the only way to stand your ground is to repeat yourself over and over again, stressing in as many different ways is necessary what it is you want to say.

You: 'I can't help you out this time.'

TOP: 'Oh, come on, it won't be too much of a bother.'

You: 'No, I can't.'

>TOP: 'Just one more time. I'll make it up to you.'
>
>You: 'No, you're not hearing me. I can't help you out this time.'
>
>TOP: 'Please. I really need you.'
>
>You: 'You need to pay attention to me. I can't do it. And I'll just stand here repeating myself until you do hear that I can't help you.'

Repeating yourself is another way of setting a boundary; if you are with someone who hears your refusal but is deliberately not accepting what you are saying, you have to set it again and again and again.

We recommend you use this tactic sparingly because it can mirror the very same tactics other people use to wear you down and you will just exacerbate someone else's frustration. It can also begin to sound quite childish after a while. We suggest judicious use of repetition.

Humour

Humour can be used to diffuse a difficult situation. A lot of nice people use clowning as a defence mechanism. That's not what we're talking about here. You can lighten up a tense situation far more effectively by seeing the humour in what's going on.

What you're looking to do is to take the heat off the situation and give yourself some breathing space.

>TOP: 'You've made a mess of this again.'
>
>You: 'Is it really that bad?'
>
>TOP: 'It's dreadful.'
>
>You: 'Oops. Goofed again. You'd better take me out and have me hung, drawn and quartered. Hanging wouldn't be good enough for me.'

Sometimes humour means jollying someone along into seeing your point of view.

> TOP: 'I don't know what you're going on about.'

> You: 'No, I can see that. Do you think we should hire a translator? Then we could get those little earphones like they have at the UN and have simultaneous translation. That might help.'

> TOP: 'Are you taking the piss?'

> You: 'I wouldn't dream of doing such a thing.'

> TOP: 'You're acting very peculiar.'

> You (Time to bring in some agreement here): 'You're right, I am peculiar. Now, let's get back to the issue at hand. Where exactly are you having problems with what I was saying? I'm sure we can work something out.'

Here is Martin's story:

> When Martin did one of our workshops he brought in a long-term problem he encountered in every job he'd had: he didn't know how to stand up for himself when it came to asking for a raise, going for a promotion, even negotiating his own office space.
>
> He was very competent at his job, but whenever he had to ask for something for himself a creeping paralysis came over him. He was quite able to defend his staff and even relished getting angry with clients or suppliers, but whenever it came to himself he just felt overwhelmed.
>
> The final straw that made him sign up for the course was this: during the week, without being consulted, he was allocated an office space he didn't want and that he felt compromised his position in his team. But, as usual,

he hadn't said anything to anyone, and bottled up huge resentments towards his colleagues and his boss.

He was convinced that if he spoke his mind, he'd be considered a troublemaker, would lose any chance for promotion anyway and he might even get fired.

Martin wanted to be able to go back to work armed with enough tools to get the decision reversed. If he was going to go back to the office after working with us and plunge into the deep end, he'd need a life jacket and some skills that wouldn't require him to alter his personality radically. Given his particular personality, humour was Martin's best defence.

He wasn't going to be able to confront or demand because that wasn't his way. What Martin learned to do was to exaggerate, in a humorous way, his feelings about what was going on.

Which is exactly what he did when he returned to work. He joked about removal men and hiring ergonomic specialists to decide the best positions for office furniture. He asked if they had got a feng shui master in to decide the best place for all the furniture. He talked about using room layouts from *Homes and Gardens* and getting in interior decorators to make sure the room was just right.

When his colleagues said he was acting strange, he said yes he was, he had taken a strange pill that morning along with his vitamins. They said he wasn't acting like himself, and he agreed, saying he'd decided to act like someone else for the day.

He didn't have to get angry or even insist they put it all back. He got their attention long enough to make his point and because he hadn't really made a huge fuss, it was harder for them to ignore his feelings. Later in the week a staff meeting was called to discuss office allocation to which Martin was invited.

Not everybody responds to humour in the way it is meant, so you do have to tread a little carefully when deciding who you use it with; but for our money, when you use humour and agreement together, you have a dynamite combo.

Objectivity

Objectivity in the face of being bullied or pressured into adapting your behaviour is quite a hard thing to accomplish. Almost impossible, if you are in the throes of being emotionally overwhelmed.

There is something you can try to give yourself some degree of objectivity, however, even if for only a short time. Next time you begin to feel under pressure, try this. Imagine yourself right outside the situation, even as it is happening. In the same way that the part of you that knows what you'd like to say is still functioning but detached from the proceedings, you can consciously detach yourself for a few seconds when you are in difficulty.

Try to look at the situation as though you were a total stranger with no hidden agenda, no vested interest, no concern about the outcome of the problem. How might that complete stranger see what's going on? If she/he wasn't stuck in the middle of your deep feelings, how would she/he view the situation? You might even ask for advice since she/he may be able to see more clearly than you.

This is really a way to trick yourself into helping yourself out, since inside us all there is an area that isn't touched by all the turmoil and can indeed 'see' the solution. Invite your 'stranger' to give you a hand.

Over-apologising

We touched on this in the chapter on language. Over-apologising is a great way to gild the lily and to bring a touch of absurdity to the proceedings. It's a kind of gentle mocking of yourself which alerts the other person to the fact that you're being tongue-in-cheek. The good thing about over-apologising is that it's an easy way to feel better when you catch yourself doing your regular apology number.

Instead of giving yourself a hard time when you hear yourself saying yet again, 'I'm sorry', you can say 'I'm sorry' and then add a few more to go with it. 'I'm so very, very sorry. You must excuse me. What must you be thinking? How awful of me.' This exaggerated grovelling helps reinforce how silly apologising is and lets the other person know that you don't really mean it.

Telling the truth

In psychotherapy jargon this is sometimes called 'levelling', and we like the whole term a lot. It is trying to get a difficult situation where someone is out-manoeuvring you back onto a 'level' keel. Levelling, or telling the truth, is just that: letting the other person know the effect they are having on you. In the conflict chapter we mentioned not using the accusatory 'you'. When you tell the truth about what is going on for you, it is a very good idea not to start sentences with 'you'. Here's an example:

> TOP: 'You know you're supposed to keep me up to date on all those files. Why do I always have to come to you to get the information, instead of the other way around?'

> You: 'I get a sinking feeling in my stomach whenever you come over to my desk so I guess I avoid coming into your office as much as I can.'

or

> TOP: 'You never ring me. I'm tired of always being the one who phones. Why can't you phone me every once in a while?'

> You: 'It feels like an attack when you talk to me like that and I get very defensive. Then I can't find the words to explain my situation. I end up making excuses that we both see through.'

Here's Andy's story:

> Andy always, but always attracted the party bore. Without fail, every time he went to a party, the most boring person in the room sought him out. Naturally, it got to the point where he stopped going to parties. But he'd get cornered at work or at the supermarket or even by the weirdos when he'd go for a walk in the park. He began expecting to get 'burgled' and resigned himself to it.
>
> His problem was that he didn't want to be rude to these people and he simply didn't know how to say he didn't want to talk to them without being rude. He thought those were his only two options: put up with it or be

insulting. This is typical: we feel we have to say nothing or else we'll go out of control and act like lunatics.

Andy had to learn the technique of politely 'levelling': letting the other person know he wasn't interested without insulting.

The next time he was invited to a party, he forced himself to go and, sure enough, a party bore came sidling up to him and began a conversation that Andy simply wasn't interested in. He took a deep breath and turned to the man and said, 'You know, none of the things you've been talking about interest me at all. I'm sure you'd do much better talking to someone else.'

He told us he was shaking inside and probably out, but it worked: the bore left him alone.

We can hear a number of you rushing to the defence of the party bore. We have discovered that that's typical. Rather than face the possibility of hurting someone else's feelings, some of you would prefer to ruin your own evening, or, as in Andy's case, stop going to parties altogether. Or you'll think of the usual excuses: 'I'm just going to get a drink; I've just seen someone I simply have to talk to; I just have to pop along to the loo.'

If you're operating out of your too nice self those excuses will come across as lame and weak and can be seen through for what they are. If your party bore is someone who is even more sensitive than you, he'll take the hint and leave you alone and the ploys will have worked.

However, if he's not, he'll tag along with you because he knows he's got someone who *appears* willing to listen to him and he's not about to let go.

The advantage to the Andys of this world of 'levelling' in such a direct way is two-fold: 1) by being so bold he gets a sense that he can actually do something he used to think was impossible; and 2) by becoming more burglar proof he'll be able to think of any number of feeble excuses and carry them off.

If you're unused to telling the truth in such a straightforward way, the phrases may seem unnecessarily hurtful. However, telling someone you're not interested saves everyone a lot of bother in the end.

We've heard of more than one instance when people went out on dates that they didn't want to go on, simply because they couldn't bear to tell the other person that they weren't interested.

The excuse is the same: I'll endure it for a little while and then it will be over.

The bottom line is that if you practise telling the truth a few times in a direct fashion, you won't be bothered any more. You will have become so much less muggable that you won't be pestered in the ways you used to be.

Giving back the problem

Nice people accept problems that other people have created – problems that often have nothing to do with them.

A friend can stand in the middle of your living room with a helpless expression on his/her face and say, 'I just don't know what I'm going to do. My Aunt Sophie is coming down from Aberdeen and I'm not sure what to do with her for five whole days.' And before you know where you are, you've said, 'I don't mind spending a day with her. I can take her to that lovely new tea shop that's opened up on the High Street.' You don t want to spend a day with Aunt Sophie. She's not your aunt. You've only met her once. It's not your problem.

If your mother sighs extravagantly and says she has to find a way to get into town so she can buy a new pair of shoes, you'll find yourself say-ing, 'That's OK, Mother, I'll find the time to take you into town.' You don't want to chauffeur your mother around; there are taxis, buses, other friends, but, no, you've accepted her problem as yours.

As a nice person it's a habit. The other person (who may or may not be doing it deliberately) announces their problem, not even asking for your help; and before you know it, you leap in, taking on their problems as your own.

There's another version where someone deliberately tries to make their problem yours. These people tend to start sentences with 'I don't know what we're going to do about...' or, 'What are we going to do about...?' It's the use of the 'we' that's key here. You're being roped in before you even know what the problem is...

TOP: 'What are we going to do about the Henderson report?'

You: 'The Henderson report?'

TOP: 'You know, it's due tomorrow and it's not completed yet. Any ideas?'

You: 'Well, I guess I could stay if you really need me to.'

And that's it for you; they got you again.

Work situations can be tricky – we know that. Quite often colleagues will try to get you involved in a project that wasn't your responsibility in the first place. When you agree to help you have to take into consideration that there might be a long-term pay-off and, therefore, you don't mind.

But if you offer to help simply because you're used to bailing people out of difficulties they get themselves into, your team spirit won't count for much. So if you are someone who gets taken in by other people's anxiety about problems they themselves created, here is how you might give the problem back without being offensive:

TOP: 'What are we going to do about the Henderson report?'

You: 'The Henderson report?'

TOP: 'You know, it's due tomorrow and it's not completed yet. Any ideas?'

You: 'I had no idea about the Henderson report. I'm sorry you didn't come to me sooner, but my mind is clear out of ideas at such late notice. I think you'll have to ask someone else who's more up-to-date with the problem.'

Aunty Rose's Vase

There are times when people are particularly horrible to you and you not only accept their bad behaviour, you let everyone you know just how upset you are about it.

Here is a metaphor that may help explain what we mean.

Ever have an Aunty Rose who gave you a really ugly vase (or its equivalent)? You hate this vase. When people come to your home you even point it out to them and tell them how ugly it is; you comment on her bad taste and how could anyone actually buy something so awful? You may even hide it away. Until Aunty Rose comes over to visit and then you dash around trying to find it so it can go on display. She never finds out that you don't like her gift at all.

This is so you won't hurt her feelings, of course. It's also so you won't feel bad yourself about telling her the truth.

If someone tells you off, yells at you, criticises you, demands things of you, manipulates you, that's the same as if they had just handed you a really ugly present that you then feel obliged to take into your home.

Not only that, just like the vase, you show it to your friends and closest confidants. You complain about how upset you are and how much the other person hurt you and made you angry. You display your feelings even though you hate having them.

You may hide the feelings away for a while, but as soon as the other person makes an appearance, out they come, as though they just happened fresh today. You will remind yourself how badly you feel. You don't really have to accept Aunty Rose's vase. You don't have to accept someone else's 'gift' of hurt, criticism, demands, manipulation.

This is your justification: how can I possibly tell Aunty Rose I don't like her vase? That's being unnecessarily cruel. It's not really a hardship to keep it in a closet till she comes over.

That same need to justify accepting someone else's bad feelings, about you will prevail: maybe they didn't know what they were doing; I couldn't possibly tell them how much they've upset me and so on.

In keeping with our metaphor, just as there are times when it might be appropriate to tell Aunty Rose that as much as you appreciate her effort, her vase simply isn't in keeping with the rest of your decorations, you need to let the other person know that their gift of manipulation or anger is also not wanted.

The most important thing in these transactions is that you don't take on extra burdens that were not yours in the first place. It's important not to act defensive when you refuse to take someone else's problem on. This is when you over-explain or over-defend why you can't do something that someone else wants you to do. Be short and sweet and hand the problem back.

Practising for when it really matters

Throughout this book we've been talking about game playing, small wins and practice. Those three areas are the crux of The Nice Factor process.

The more small wins you accumulate the better prepared you are when something difficult arises. The best way to collect wins is to practise when the outcome doesn't matter. If you confront one of your big difficulties head on without having gained some confidence in your ability to handle the situation, you are likely to revert back to old habits and feel a failure. That's because the outcome matters, you care about what happens.

However, there are many situations you will find yourself in where there is no outcome, where there are no consequences and it doesn't matter what happens one way or the other.

When you're in the middle of strong or difficult feelings about something, it is not a good time to practise. If there are no feelings attached to the situation other than a sense of excitement and play because you might be doing something difficult, that's the perfect time to go into a plan of action.

How do you create a plan of action? How do you refine your own personal art of saying no?

Here are a few more suggestions of ways you can practise when there will be no consequences, no one will know you're doing it except you. You'll be playing life like a game.

These are situations in which you can quietly but firmly make a deliberate choice to do something other than what you would normally do. You can deliberately choose to alter, adapt and modify your behaviour to suit you and because there is nothing but your choice at stake, it doesn't matter. They are everyday situations that might wrong-foot you if you were taken unawares.

The restaurant scenario

Sending something back if it isn't the way you want when you're eating out can be difficult. The soup may not be warm enough, your main course overdone or the pudding disappointing, but, because this is one of those areas where your niceness takes over, you won't want to make a fuss or insult the chef or, even worse, have someone question your difficulty.

If you are one of these people, the next time you go into a restaurant, and *there is absolutely nothing wrong whatsoever*, make something up. It doesn't have to be major. You could ask for more bread, an extra glass of water, another serviette: anything will do, because it won't matter. You can even practise changing your mind and calling the waiter or waitress back and telling them you've decided on a different starter.

This is practising when it doesn't matter. You're not having the same sort of difficult feelings in the way you would if there really was a problem. Practise when there isn't one.

No questions asked

Perhaps you're someone who finds it hard to return something once you've bought it, even if it's flawed in some way or if you decide you don t like it. Go into one of the stores with a no-questions-asked refund policy and deliberately buy something you don't want for the express purpose of returning it. Get into practice for when it really matters.

Many of these stores train their staff to be extra nice to customers who return goods; some of them even advertise their policy as a major selling point in shopping at their store. Take advantage of it. It won't matter. No one will know you're doing it but you. It's a chance to do something that you would find difficult if you opened the packet and found the blouse/shirt stained, the trousers too short or that you hated the jacket after all.

If you buy something you genuinely don't want, in order to return it, as an exercise in being not nice, it's another win.

Nice/not nice days

These days are arbitrarily chosen.

How about: Have a nice day?

Today I'm going to have a nice day. I'm going to be sweetness and light to everyone who comes near me. They won't know what hit them as they drown in treacle, I'll be so nice. The more people I get to smile, the higher my score is on that day.

or

How about: Have a not nice day?

Today I'm going to operate in the Middle Ground the entire day, no matter what the situation. This means I'm going to be direct, forthright and up-front. I'm going to ask for what I want; I'm going to set clear boundaries; I'm not going to apologise for anything.

How about a day off?

You don't need to practise this stuff every day. Give yourself a break. There will be days when you will want to hide under the duvet and not come out. So don't. You don't have to be not nice all the time: you can hide out and be nice and weak and wimpy and pathetic. You can give in to everyone and accommodated your behaviour just as you always did. The difference is that you're doing it by choice: it's your day off.

Conclusion

We've covered a lot of ground looking at ways you can alter your behaviour to become less nice, how to develop saying no in ways where the word is never or hardly ever used. Some of the suggestions may seem easy to you and others may feel too difficult to tackle just now.

If you think back to how you acquired a particular skill, such as driving, swimming, speaking a foreign language, etc, you were uncoordinated and not very good at it in the beginning. You had to practise hill starts till you stopped rolling back, splash around in the shallow end till you could stay afloat and coordinate the strokes at the same time, and say everything in the present tense until you mastered all the others.

The key word here is practise. You had to practise, sometimes for a long time, sometimes for a little, but practise is what you had to do. You've been practising nice behaviour for the better part of your life. You're very good at it. If you decide that becoming less nice is important, you're going to have to practise that as well. It's no good picking up a violin when you've never had any lessons expecting to play an Irish jig or a Tchaikovsky concerto.

In the same way not niceness isn't just going to happen by reading this book. It certainly isn't going to happen overnight. A woman who did our very first Nice Factor workshop spoke to us about six months later and said she realised that she *grew* into being not nice. We like that image and encourage everyone who decides to take on our work to look at it in those terms: it's something to grow into.

It's certain that if you practise some of the simpler tactics first and accumulate your storehouse of small wins, you will be better equipped to deal with the major issues of your life *when you decide you are ready to.*

So have fun and play with the material in the book; indeed, play life more as a game where you may be the only player but where you have quite a few aces up your sleeve. We encourage you to have patience with yourself and to score as a win making an attempt at new behaviour (whether you succeed or not).

When you return the shoes, ask for more bread, change your answering machine message, exaggerate your apologies, act like a 'ten' one day and a 'one' the next, you gain more experience, not in being nice or nasty, but in being more yourself.

For that, ultimately, is what this book and our workshops are all about: helping you get back to the you you'd like to be. The you that knew what you wanted, expressed your feelings freely and had a spontaneous response to the world.

We hope that by reading this book you have found ways to bring the inner you and the external you closer together. We hope you have seen that changing your behaviour can be a fun process, rather than a burden. We hope you will enjoy saying no in new ways.

Nice people make the world a pleasanter place to be and we wouldn't want you to lose any of the *qualities* that make up your personality. This book is a guide and a support for changing your behaviour, not changing the essence of who you are.

Fin

That will do nicely, thank you.

THE ART OF SAYING NO: RECAPITULATION

Putting It All Together or Am I Allowed To Do That?

Here's a 'crib sheet' to remind you of some of the ideas and suggestions we have included in the book. We have extracted a precis of hints and tips that you can use as a quick reference when you're not too sure what would be the best thing for you to do in a particular situation.

Stay conscious

The more aware you are of your behaviour, feelings, needs and wants, the more you can do something to change them, even if not right away. Noticing what you do and how you feel is already a win, rather than the win being the change.

Staying conscious includes being aware of your:

- Feelings: What emotions sweep over you when you are confronted with a situation you feel is out of your control? What feelings get in the way of being able to do what you want rather than what other people want from you?
- Physicality: What is your body language telling people about you? What do you actually do when you are being too nice?
- Language: What comes out of your mouth when you are being too nice? Identifying your 'language of adaptation' will help you to make small changes right away.

Give your brain a break

Your poor brain works overtime to make things up for you. You then act as though they are true. Your inner life is littered with assumptions that may or may not be true, but because you are convinced they are, you gear much of your behaviour to those assumptions. The only way to know if an assumption is true is to ask. If you don't know, you'd be better off assuming the exact opposite of what you've made up. You have just as much chance of being right and you're making assumptions in your favour, instead of the other person's.

Choice

Keep in mind that you always have a choice. There are times when it may not feel like it, but whatever you decide to do, make it a choice, even if it's to be too nice. Knowing you have chosen keeps you in charge of your own actions.

Playing life like a game

Having fun with raising your awareness and changing your behaviour. As you are the only player in the game, no one knows what you are doing except you. You can play the game full out, you can quit mid-way through or you can not play at all.

Small wins

Becoming less nice isn't going to happen overnight. You don't have to be perfect at this – you won't be. Start collecting small wins to build your self-confidence and self-esteem.

Dos and don'ts

Here is a list of methods, techniques and tactics we've suggested throughout the book that are designed to support you in your quest to become less nice and more fully yourself.

Not smiling

Smiling is a dead give-away that you're trying to soften the message. It gives permission for someone to think you don't really mean what you say because you've got this big grin on your face. They can tell themselves that really, deep down, you like what they're doing. It is important for you to take yourself as seriously as you want others to take you.

Maintaining eye contact
This is very hard for some people, to be able to look someone in the eye for any length of time. Looking away tends to imply that you're not really interested in pursuing the subject. If someone can't see your face clearly, they don't know exactly how genuine your words are.

Standing your ground
Backing off just doesn't work. It's wishy-washy. It gives no signal of what your intentions are. The other person may not even realise you're doing it and will simply adjust the space to how they want it. Standing your ground gives weight to your intention. This means both physically standing your ground and verbally standing your ground.

Speaking in a firm voice
Not necessarily loud, a common mistake. You don't have to yell to let people know what you want, but the words do have to be firm and strong to convey that you really mean it.

Telling the truth
This is letting the other person know what you are feeling. It's 'levelling' with them that you aren't comfortable with what they are doing or saying. This can be difficult because revealing how you feel may make you feel quite vulnerable. It's good for boundary setting and conflict resolution: it makes your position very clear.

Not rising to the bait
You can get sucked into having conversations you don't want to have because you try to reason with the other person. Then the other person can dangle a seemingly irrefutable argument in front of you and you're hooked. Remember to be a wise old trout on the bottom of the lake.

Agreement
If someone tells you you're being silly, agree with them. They have no place to go after that. 'You're being a bit touchy, aren't you?' 'Yes, you're

right, I am.' It takes the wind out of their sails and wrong-foots them for a change. This can be a lot of fun to play with.

Not blaming or accusing
If you intend telling someone you don't like their behaviour, start sentences with how you feel, not what's wrong with them. Pointing an accusatory finger will only make them more defensive and less willing to listen to what you have to say.

Moving the argument forward
Making sure the discussion, argument or quarrel actually goes somewhere instead of on a tape loop, repeating the same old arguments you've always had. This may mean calling a 'time-out' to stop the treadmill and get the discussion back on a track that s going somewhere.

Bridge building
Give something to the other person so that they'll want to give something to you in return. You may simply be offering tea and sympathy, but it could be enough to turn the tide in your favour.

Finding out why you can't have what you want
There may be many good reasons why someone can't give you what you'd like. Gentle probing to find out why can be your win. Then you could move on to…

Changing what you do want
Finding out why you can't have what you want doesn't mean you can't have anything. Changing your want to being thanked and praised will allow the other person to give you something and you to take away a small gift and a small win.

Buying time
There are a number of small things you can do to create enough breathing space to get your feelings of upset or panic under control. Keep a list of excuses handy (including the loose hyena) to get yourself out of situations long enough to see clearly what's going on before you put yourself back in the fray.

Slowing the pace

Use silence or short, punchy sentences to make your point. If someone is creating a gap in the hope that you'll fill it by offering help or a solution, grab hold of your impulse to fill it. Let the other person be uncomfortable for a change.

Getting your 'no' in quickly

Set your marker right at the beginning of the discussion. You can aways change your mind later, but if you say it fast, it's out on the table and can't be ignored.

Wait a minute

A good little phrase to use when you want to back-track on something you've said or done that you know isn't quite right. 'I'm sorry. Wait a minute! No, I'm not.' It alerts both yourself and the other person that you need to stop and reassess. This, of course, leads to the possibility that you might be...

Changing your mind

You have the right to change your mind, whether it's two minutes, two hours, two months or two years after the fact. However much you've been told to honour your commitments, there will be times when you aren't able to or don't want to.

Not engaging

Never apologise, never explain. Don't supply fuel for the other person to use against you.

Keeping things short and sweet

Gabbling won't help, it just gives the other person rope to hang you with. When you have something to say, keep it as short as possible.

Offering lots of options

Rather than saying an outright 'no', you can explain that although you can't help out, there may be a solution that doesn't involve you. The more options you offer, the fewer opportunities the other person has to insist it has to be you.

Repeating yourself

Repeating yourself enough times to ensure that the other person has got the message is another form of standing your ground. To be used with caution since you might get yourself strangled in the process.

Humour

Finding the humour in the current event in order to relieve some of the tension and defuse a difficult situation. Humour is a way to protect yourself from having to take on someone else's view of the seriousness of a problem.

Over-apologising

Gilding the lily, going over the top, playing it for all it's worth. You can use your nice language and behaviour to the hilt and have lots of fun grovelling to make your point. Goes well with humour and agreeing.

Objectivity

Trying to see the problem, confrontation or conflict from an objective point of view. Looking at the situation as though you were an outsider with no vested interest in the outcome.

Giving back the problem

This is another form of not engaging or rising to the bait. It can be used when someone presents you with a problem that's theirs and not yours and covertly expects you to solve it for them; or when they try to rope you in on their problem and overtly expect you to get involved. Standing back and letting them find their own solution is best.

Playing the status game

Here is a reminder of the qualities that we associate with high- or low-status behaviour. Using status manipulation as a tool is a great way to change your behaviour without thought. On a whim.

Remember that a lot of status play is about closing the tension gap that other people create in order to manipulate and manoeuvre you into doing what they want.

Playing a 'ten': positive aspects of high-status behaviour

- Be physically higher than the other person.
- Take your time.
- Use silence.
- Stand tall, shoulders back.
- Speak in a very deliberate, firm voice.
- Repeat yourself.
- Listen without comment.
- Be above the argument.
- Stand your ground.
- Maintain strong eye contact.
- Avoid getting side-tracked by superfluous arguments.
- Make no excuses, offer no explanations.
- Have very clear boundaries.

Playing a 'one': positive aspects of low-status behaviour

- Physically get on the same level or lower than the other person.
- Speak in a low, sympathetic voice.
- Exhibit lots of empathy and understanding.
- Acknowledge the other person's feelings.
- Be sad or disappointed on their behalf.
- Look down.
- Use sympathetic body posture.
- Overdo apology and niceness.
- Also have very clear boundaries.

Status reversal
This is particularly useful when dealing with parents or any situation when the status gap is very wide.

- Avoid making the other person feel they are wrong or try to convince them that you're right.
- Be as patient as is humanly possible.
- Listen to what the other person is saying and acknowledge their feelings.

- Avoid getting drawn into childish arguments.
- Avoid explaining the unexplainable.
- Avoid accusing the other person of trying to control your life, which is probably what it feels like.
- Avoid playing verbal ping-pong.
- Keep returning to things that you want to talk about.

Changing Yourself In Order To Change Others

Everything we have included in this recap, as is true for the whole book, is to help you change you in order to make things different as opposed to hoping all the other people will change and make your life easier. This is what it means to be more in charge of your life. If you expect others to do all the work, they will still be in control of what happens. This is all about moving from a victim mentality to an action mentality and taking a firm hold of the reins of your life.

Then you simply have to…

Practise, Practise, Practise

We cannot emphasise enough how important it is for you to accept that you aren't going to change your behaviour overnight. By practising some of the techniques, the art, if you will, in this book you will grow into becoming less nice. You will find out which tactics suit you and which ones don't. Making mistakes is inevitable. Look on the try as a win and keep on practising.

Remember some of the easy places where we suggested practising: in a pub, at a zebra crossing, walking down your high street, in a restaurant, at a shop with a no-questions-asked refund policy. Practise on your best friend, practise in front of the mirror, practise with your most loving pet.

Just keep on practising.

About The Authors

Robin Chandler and Jo Ellen Grzyb are the directors of Impact Factory, which is a professional personal development company, located in London. Impact Factory runs Assertiveness workshops on a regular basis throughout the year. For more information on Impact Factory programmes contact:

www.impactfactory.com
or
Impact Factory
Suite 121 Business Design Centre
52 Upper Street
London N1 0QH
Phone: +44 (0) 20 7226 1877
Fax: +44 (0) 20 7354 3505

Jo Ellen Grzyb is also the author of *Family Heaven, Family Hell: How to Survive the Family Get Together* (www.familyheavenfamilyhell.com).